A
Taste
of
Eden

A
Taste
of
Eden

(More) Torah for the
Shabbat Table

Rabbi Ari D. Kahn

KODESH PRESS

A Taste of Eden
More Torah for the Shabbat Table
© Ari D. Kahn 2016
978-0-9978205-4-6

Cover Art Courtesy of Ofra Friedland
www.ofrafriedland.co.il

Published & Distributed by
Kodesh Press L.L.C.
New York, NY
www.KodeshPress.com
kodeshpress@gmail.com

This volume is
dedicated in honor of

Elizabeth Gindi
Joleen Julis

and

Naomi Kahn

Table of Contents

Sefer Bereishit

Sefer Shemot

9

A Taste of Eden

Sefer Vayikra

Sefer Bemidbar

A Taste of Eden

Sefer Devarim

Introduction

The Shabbat is the time when there is a mystical meeting between the Jewish people and the Shekhinah. The Talmud (*Bava Kamma* 32) recounts how the sages would go out and welcome the bride/queen Shabbat.

When we welcome the Shabbat we say the words *bo'i kallah*, "Welcome, bride." Shabbat is a time of family, and a time spirituality.

How appropriate to dedicate this volume to some very special women who represent the Shekhinah in our respective homes.

I once gain have the distinct honor to thank Elizabeth and Raymond Gindi, and Joleen and Mitch Julis; who have partnered with me in this work as well as my previous works.

This concept of writing succinct, but hopefully timely relevant works with a contemporary message was Mitch's idea, and based on the response, he was apparently quite visionary.

A special thanks to the incomparable Ofra Friedland, who has graciously allowed her artwork to adorn this volume.

A Taste of Eden

Thanks to Rabbi Alec Goldstein of Kodesh Press for his professionalism and friendship.

It is my hope that this volume will help bring spirituality to the Shabbat meals, and will be an appropriate companion to the soulful meals prepared by women and men the world over, and make the Shekhinah manifest.

Special thanks to Matityahu & Shira & Kedem, Hillel, Yishai, Yosef & Shoval, and Elisheva, who make our Shabbat table, lively interesting and tasteful in every way.

To Naomi, my best reader, editor, audience and friend, for all you do and how you do it.

Ari Kahn
Tu B'Av 5776
Givat Ze'ev

Parashat Bereishit
The Shabbat App

Heaven and earth, and all their components, were [thus] completed. With the seventh day, God finished all the work that He had done. He [thus] ceased on the seventh day from all the work that He had been doing. God blessed the seventh day, and He declared it to be holy, for it was on this day that God ceased from all the work that He had been creating [so that it would continue] to function. (*Bereishit* 2:1-3)

The Torah begins with the ultimate paradigm shift: Creation of our physical universe, and then rest. In a concise, even cryptic few verses, our existence, our world, and our place in that world, come into being. Time, space, and matter come into existence; the cosmos takes shape. Life springs forth, and man, the first sentient, self-aware being, is introduced. From the moment of *Bereishit*, Genesis, everything else is, quite literally, history. Mankind is endowed with both physical and spiritual capabilities, and is given the freedom to put those capabilities to use—for better or worse: To work and protect the Garden, to rule over all of nature and harness its great power, while remaining mindful of our tremendous responsibilities and capabilities.

A Taste of Eden

The Torah describes other paradigm shifts, and from our vantage point we are able to identify critical moments in human and Jewish history that might be considered new beginnings: Abraham's message of monotheism and the Revelation at Sinai are two such moments. But what of our more recent history?

It is unclear, for example, whether or not people who lived through it were aware that what we now call "the Industrial Revolution" was breaking out all around them. Did they realize that the world would be changed forever by the breakthroughs of their time? The onset of this "revolution" is often difficult to pinpoint: Was it the invention of the cotton gin or the invention of the steam engine that began the ever-accelerating leaps and bounds of invention? Whatever that first step may have been, it is clear to us that the advancement of technology brought about a massive paradigm shift. Emerging technologies gave humankind new tools, but also changed our perception of the world, of our place in it, and of life itself. It is altogether likely, though, that at the time, the changes were perceived as local and limited. The full impact, import, and implications of each new invention may not have been grasped by those who were closest to it; the pace at which new inventions and technology appeared, each one building upon the one before it, was dizzying.

This Industrial Revolution has not abated ever since; it has morphed into the technological revolution that is unfolding all around us, to the point that in our own lifetimes we have become capable of holding in the palms of our hands (often for far too many hours a day) technological power that was beyond imagination when the "revolution" first began.

"Smart phones," which are actually small computers with access to the worldwide reservoir of knowledge, make the

Parashat Bereishit

path to limitless information direct and virtually uninhibited. In addition, countless "apps" have been developed to organize and optimize our access to a web of facts, opinions, and ideas. While some of these apps serve as mere diversions, many others perform and monitor tasks that can make us more informed, in-touch, productive, and efficient than ever before.

Recently, a "Shabbat app" was reportedly developed, which promises to solve the "problem" of the cruel isolation experienced by Sabbath-observant Jews for 25 hours every week.

The technical, micro-halachic considerations that would either support or prohibit the use of this app, based upon an examination of the inner workings of the app itself or the device on which it would operate, are beyond the scope of this forum. Instead, I would like to address the larger issues involved—what we may call "macro-halachic considerations."

A micro-halachic analysis measures any new technology in terms of its alignment with the 39 categories of productive labor listed in the Mishnah. Each of these 39 prohibited categories, and the sub-categories that are extrapolated from them, are the stuff and substance of the biblical prohibition of productive work on the Sabbath. On the other hand, macro-halachic considerations are based on the positive, proactive commandment, "On the seventh day, you shall rest."

Whereas the 39 prohibited categories of labor are detailed and precise, the positive commandment, to create a Sabbath environment, is far more amorphous, and its content and contours have been entrusted to the rabbis. The job of the rabbis has been perceived as the preservation of the spirit of Shabbat, particularly when adherence to the letter of the law allows the spirit of Shabbat to be trampled upon. In such cases, rabbinic mandate has been exercised by creating legal safeguards that protect the spirit of Shabbat. One particularly famous and well-documented case of the exercise of this rabbinic mandate was that of a rabbi named Isaiah, better known as the Prophet Isaiah. Isaiah, who lived over 2500 years ago, issued a far-reaching and bold halachic decision requiring all Jews to close their stores on Shabbat. In point of fact, there was no technical, legal prohibition against leaving one's shop open on Shabbat; a store could be left open without breaking any Torah laws. There was no planting or harvesting involved, nor any other activity that was expressly prohibited. Commerce, per se, violated no Torah laws. On the other hand, Isaiah understood that conducting commerce on Shabbat is an affront to the holy day of rest, as it undermines the spirit of the day even if it violates no specific injunction.

On a theoretical level, Sabbath observance in the modern world should be exponentially easier than ever before in history. Technology makes it possible to live in comfort, even luxury, without the need to perform any of the work prohibited on Shabbat. Unfortunately, man has become enslaved to the very technology designed to liberate him. Our technological creations have risen up and are poised to overcome us, like Frankenstein's monster or a golem of our own design. We are addicted to the constant flow of communication that we have created. We have become incapable of functioning without our virtual community, without our constant access to the information we ourselves produce. We do not allow ourselves one day each week to reconnect with our inner selves, our souls, our God. We find it more and more difficult to pray with the

Parashat Bereishit

distraction of tweets, beeps, and blips. We are rapidly losing our ability to sit around the table, to make eye-contact with loved ones or guests, to engage in and foster actual, not virtual, communication, to nurture love and respect. We are at risk of forgetting the most basic and human of all arts: the art of communication and attentive listening.

Rather than searching for ways to sidestep Shabbat's prohibitions, we should follow in the footsteps of Isaiah, and seek out new ways to enhance and deepen our Shabbat experience. The proper use of the Shabbat app, if and when it is made available, is exclusively for people working in emergency or security positions: Physicians, army, and police personnel, or others who are required to sidestep (but choose not to disregard) the 39 prohibited categories of labor on Shabbat. For the rest of us, instead of strengthening the stranglehold technology has on our lives, instead of allowing technology to take over our Shabbat as it has the other six days of the week, instead of increasing our servitude to 24/7, we should be marketing the benefits of a gadget-free Shabbat to all members of modern society. Rather than an app that would give technology a foothold on Shabbat, I would welcome an app that shuts down our devices during meals, prayers, and during the precious time we spend with our loved ones, even on weekdays. This app would be a beneficial tool indeed.

If you restrain your foot, because of the Sabbath, from pursuing your business on My holy day; and call the Sabbath a delight, the holy day of the honorable God; if you honor it, not doing your own ways, nor pursuing your own business, nor speaking of vain matters; Then

A Taste of Eden

shall you delight in God, and I will cause you to ride upon the high places of the earth, and sustain you with the heritage of Jacob your father; for the mouth of God has spoken. (Isaiah 58:13-14)

Parashat Noach
Men Behaving Very Badly

The hope of a brand new world was quickly shattered. Sin eclipsed holiness, and almost immediately, Adam and Eve were evicted from Eden. They had eaten the fruit of the one tree that had been forbidden to them. The sin, and its punishment, are both clear and unequivocal.

The sin of Cain, though far more devastating, is somewhat less straightforward: He took a life, but it is not clear if his act of fratricide violated an explicit commandment. While it should have been self-evident to him, as it should be to all of us, that murder—particularly of one's own flesh and blood—is a sin of unparalleled magnitude, we may nonetheless imagine that a good defense attorney would have an easier time defending Cain. Adam and Eve defied God's explicit instructions; they could not plead ignorance or incompetence.

But what of the generation of the flood, in which all of creation was found guilty and sentenced to annihilation? Their behavior was quite corrupt, but did they, in fact, break any "laws"? Was their sin like that of Adam and Eve, a flagrant violation of God's explicit directive, or were they more like Cain, who was expected to have an innate appreciation for the sanctity of human life?

A Taste of Eden

While the preamble to the flood speaks of a society riddled with corruption and violence, the Torah provides the backdrop for the situation, giving us insight into the state of mind that created this corrupt and violent society.

> Man began to increase on the face of the earth, and daughters were born to them. The sons of the powerful [*bnei elohim*] saw that the daughters of man were good, and they took themselves wives from whomever they chose. (*Bereishit* 6:1-2)

The inequity is stark and unmistakable: Here we have the first power struggle in history. This is no mere patriarchy; it is a society based on power and victimization. *Bnei elohim*, the sons of the mighty and powerful, took the daughters—the most vulnerable offspring of lowly, weak, pedestrian man.

How different this is from the description of Adam's union with Eve:

> The man said, "Now this is bone from my bones and flesh from my flesh. She shall be called woman [*ishah*] because she was taken from man [*ish*]. Therefore, man shall leave his father and mother and be united with his wife, and they shall become one flesh. (*Bereishit* 2:23-24)

Adam does not objectify Eve; they come together as equals.

> The man and his wife were both naked, but they were not embarrassed. (*Bereishit* 2:25)

Parashat Noach

In only a few generations, man's moral deterioration is drastic, and it is rooted in the objectification of women. Powerful men regarded women in unnatural terms, not as equals but as commodities. They saw that "the daughters of man were good," and they "took" them, like so much property. Women were not courted or serenaded; no chocolates or flowers were offered, no poetry read. These were not marriages between soulmates. Men did not extol the virtues of leaving their parents' homes in order to create new families. In this society, a man simply dragged the weaker women by the hair back to his cave. The description is cold and violent, and imparts no more regard for women than would be afforded any other object: "And they took themselves wives from whomever they chose."

This behavior was both indecent and displeasing to God; in addition, it may very likely have been a violation of a Divine commandment that lies at the heart of the creation of mankind.

On the sixth day, God made an announcement concerning the creation of man:

> And the Almighty said, "Let us make man in our image and likeness...." (*Bereishit* 1:26)

To whom did God address this declaration? So many commentaries have suggested solutions to this textual challenge. Was it the heavens and the earth that the Almighty invited to take part in the creation of man? Was it the angels? This declaration is immediately followed by a description of the act of creation itself, using a very specific term that denotes *ex nihilo* creation, the creation of something from nothingness, of which only God is capable. Whereas the declaration uses the term "make"

A Taste of Eden

(*naaseh*), the act of creation itself that immediately follows is described as *va-yivra*, "and God created." To make matters even more interesting, in the following chapter, the creation of man is described as "formation" (*va-yitzer*), which denotes the use of preexisting matter.

These three different verbs are extremely precise, and very different from one another. God's first act is *ex nihilo* creation of the human form, *va-yivra*. But this creation is not complete: At a later stage, God imbues this human form with a soul. He breathes into man a part of His spirit, transforming the purely physical being into something more than the sum of its physical components. This is the act of *va-yitzer*, which makes use of preexisting physical and spiritual components. What, then, do we learn from the declaration God made before this process began? What is the meaning of *naaseh adam*, "let us make man"?

God's declaration, His "invitation," actually reveals an astonishing possibility: God called upon man himself, even before his creation—to take part in the making of man.[1] The image in which man is created, and in which he is invited to become an active participant, is the image of God reflected in the Divine Name of *Elohim*, meaning "Almighty," and possessing all powers. The Almighty God invites man, who is endowed with tremendous physical, intellectual, and spiritual capabilities, to manifest this image of God, using these capabilities to create a just and stable society and rule over all of creation. It is these same capabilities that tempt man to subjugate and control others, to exert power and violence in a destructive manner, yet God, who is all-powerful, invites man to manifest the image of God within him, to be creative and use his capabilities to build

1. See comments of *Bechor Shor* on *Bereishit* 1:26.

24

Parashat Noach

and improve the world. God's invitation, "Let us make man in our image and likeness," is a declaration of intent that is the very foundation of the act of creation that will follow. It is an invitation to mankind to take part in creation by taking part in the perfection of human society and thus bringing the image of God within us to its full expression.

When the men of the generation of the flood used their power to dominate the weak, they rebelled against this first commandment, *Let us make man in our image and likeness.* When powerful men saw women as "goods," objectifying their bodies and ignoring their souls, they turned their backs on the image of God that is the foundation of the creation of mankind.

The Torah recounts the creation of man as a three-step process: First, *bri'ah*—creation of the human form in an act of *ex nihilo*, Divine will. Next, *yetzirah*—the formation of man as a spiritual being, infusing the physical form with the breath of God. And finally, there is the 'making of man,' a process which has been ongoing since the very dawn of history, a commandment that we must strive to fulfill each and every day. We are commanded to use our capabilities to create—to build and improve, to create partnerships and communities, families and friendships. We must never use our power to exploit or enslave others. This moral imperative is older than mankind; it is the declaration of intent with which mankind was created, and it is embodied in God's invitation to us all to be active partners in creation: "Let us make man in our image and likeness."

The generation of the flood abused their capabilities, and violated this most basic commandment. For this reason, they forfeited their right to exist. Like a giant *mikveh*, the cleansing waters of the flood "reset" the world and washed away the cruel and corrupt society they had created.

A Taste of Eden

Fortunately for us, God vowed that He would never again bring a flood of these proportions upon the world. This does not indicate that the world does not deserve this punishment; in fact, we are far more similar to the generation of the flood than we would like to admit. Yet despite our own failures, God voluntarily removed this type of total eradication from His arsenal; He disabled the restart button, as it were. In order to teach mankind not to abuse the power with which we are endowed, God states that He too will not use His limitless power in this way.

And yet, powerful men and women continue to abuse their capabilities. As individuals and societies, we continue to misuse our own power. As we read the Torah, we would do well to remind ourselves that the image of God in which we are created gives us the ability to rise to the challenge of the very first commandment; indeed—*let us make man!*

Parashat Lech Lecha
Luminosity

Great people are made, not born. Sometimes they are self-made. Avraham was such a person. Born into the dark ages when decency was not common, he alone discovered the light and shared it with the world. His legacy is not merely the impact he had on his contemporaries, nor is he to be judged only by the deeds he performed in his lifetime. Quite the opposite is true: In his hometown, he was reviled. In his lifetime, the scope of his impact was limited, yet his teachings have spread throughout the world and throughout history. Jews, Muslims, and Christians all over the world look to Avraham as their spiritual, if not biological, patriarch. Regrettably, there are times that it seems that the greatness of Avraham is one of the few things upon which these religions can agree.

Rabbi Yosef Dov Soloveitchik once referred to Avraham as the "loneliest man who ever lived," the original "lonely man of faith." Avraham's greatness lay in his ability to see beyond societal beliefs and norms, and search for a truth that had eluded his contemporaries, but being the only man who believed in a deity with no needs, no appetites or desires made Avraham a loner. The concept of such a God befuddled the pagans and

A Taste of Eden

appalled their primitive logic, which required gods who could be manipulated and bribed.

Avraham's understanding of God led him to the realization that the creation of our world and of humankind was an act of benevolence and altruism. As soon as Avraham realized this, he knew there was, in fact, nothing he could do for God—so he set out to emulate God. And as he built his life around acts of kindness and morality, something magical happened: People responded. Love and decency became contagious. Talk of one God, all-powerful and without needs, began to spread. The lonely Avraham became popular. He gained a following; yet despite the inroads he made into the surrounding society, his success was limited. Even those closest to him—his nephew Lot and his son Yishmael—found the standards set by Avraham's living example too difficult to emulate. Avraham remained *ha-Ivri,* the man perpetually set apart from others, always different, as if a river separated him from the rest of society. In modern parlance, he was always "on the wrong side of the tracks."

Despite the experiences of his own lifetime, from the vantage point we enjoy, Avraham's profound loneliness was only a temporary state: God Himself became Avraham's greatest companion. God took Avraham for a stroll and invited him to look at the beautiful night sky, bright with the light of millions of stars. Avraham was told that one day his descendants would be like the stars. Indeed, this promise has been fulfilled not only in a quantitative sense, but in a qualitative sense: Avraham's descendants brought light to the darkness, compassion and altruism to the dark ages of paganism and barbarism. Avraham's followers taught kindness, decency and love, and illuminated the darkness of the human condition. Like the beauty of the

Parashat Lech Lecha

stars on a dark night, Avraham's descendants fill the sky. And the most luminous light of all, the brightest guiding star, was Avraham himself—the father of love and light.

Parashat Vayera
It Never Crossed My Mind

The killing of any child is grotesque, the killing of one's own child, obscene. But the challenge of *Akeidat Yitzchak* ("The Binding of Isaac"), in which God calls upon Avraham to bring his beloved son as an offering, is compounded when we recall all the years that Avraham and Sarah waited for the birth of this child. It seems cruel to finally give this elderly, devout couple a child—only to take him away. And if the child must die, death at the hands of his gentle father is unfathomable. Avraham, after all, is the paragon of *chesed*, the first to have recognized God as the source of loving-kindness. From Avraham and Sarah's perspective, God's request seems unspeakably cruel. Even worse, in light of the covenant God had made with Avraham, this new commandment seems impossible, outrageous, absurd: God had promised that Yitzchak would be the progeny through which the covenant would come to fruition. Calling for Yitzchak's death is illogical. Nonetheless, Avraham is prepared to fulfill God's instructions, without question or hesitation.

From our own perspective, the commandment to sacrifice Yitzchak does not sit any better. Subsequent portions of the Torah and Prophets contain powerful polemics against human sacrifice and particularly child sacrifice. The "test" which God

Parashat Vayera

throws as a gauntlet before Avraham not only goes against our most basic human emotions and sensibilities, but it also contravenes God's own laws.

All of this makes this one of the most difficult episodes in the Torah. So much discussion and debate and so much spilt ink have been dedicated to this section of our *parashah* over the generations that it is easy to lose sight of some of its most important aspects. Let us consider some of the critical background information we all know, but tend to overlook in the face of God's shocking request. First, we should read the text very carefully, to re-sensitize ourselves to what is there—and what is not.

At no point in the narrative of the *Akeidah* does God command Avraham to bind Yitzhak, nor is there any mention of taking his life. While this may seem like semantic nitpicking, it is important to note that up to this point in the Torah, Avraham had constructed other altars to God, but had never sacrificed anything on these altars. Perhaps our familiarity with later sacrificial practices unnecessarily colors our reading of this text.

Another important element is the introduction to the entire episode: "After these events, God tested Avraham." In fact, it seems that Avraham knows that he is being tested. How else are we to understand Avraham's complete silence in this most extreme situation, when in previous episodes he was so outspoken on behalf of those he perceived as innocent victims? In the previous chapter, when Sarah demands that Avraham's son Yishmael be banished, Avraham is quite troubled; here, there is no mention that Avraham experiences distress of any kind. When Avraham is told that the city of Sodom is to be destroyed, he engages God in elaborate negotiations, and stops just short of accusing God of committing injustice. Avraham's silence now, when his beloved son is to be brought as an offering, speaks volumes.

We must conclude that Avraham knows much more than we do: Avraham knows that this is a test—and he rises to the challenge.

There is something else that Avraham knows: He, too, was "sacrificed" by his own father. According to the Midrash, Avraham was thrust into a fiery furnace—and escaped unscathed. In fact, this is a central element of Avraham's relationship with God: "I am God who took you out of Ur [the fire] of Casdim" (*Bereishit* 15:7). God rescued Avraham when Terah handed him over to Nimrod to be killed for spreading monotheism and rejecting the idolatry and paganism of the society in which he was raised.

Having experienced salvation from a near-death experience, and knowing that God is just and faithful to His word, Avraham sensed that he was being tested. He saw no need to engage God in debate. This was not like Sodom, a corrupt and violent society that, in fact, had earned its death sentence and could only be saved if Avraham interceded. The case of Yitzchak was completely different than that of Sodom, or of Yishmael: God had made a covenant with Avraham, and Avraham had no doubt that the story would have a "happy ending." Just as he had been saved from death, so would Yitzchak; if God had saved him, a young former-pagan who had no covenant, surely Yitzchak, a monotheist and the son of a monotheist, and the subject of a holy covenant to boot, would be saved as well.

Yitzchak's death was never a possibility—not as far as Avraham was concerned, and not as far as God was concerned.

Parashat Vayera

God's commandment to Avraham was very specific, and Avraham understood it very precisely: Yitzchak was to be "raised up as an offering," and God would use the opportunity to teach humankind, once and for all, that human sacrifice, child sacrifice, is not acceptable.

This is precisely how the sages of the Talmud (*Taanit* 4a) understood *Akeidat Yitzchak*. Citing the Prophet Jeremiah's exhortation against child sacrifice (Chapter 19), they state unequivocally that such behavior "never crossed God's mind," referring specifically to the sacrificial slaughter of Yitzchak.

Though readers of this *parashah* throughout the generations have been disturbed, even horrified, by the *Akeidah*, there was no miscommunication between God and Avraham. The thought of actually killing Yitzchak never crossed their minds.

Parashat Hayei Sarah
Negotiations and Acquisitions

A strange negotiation is reported in this week's *parashah*. Sarah has died, and Avraham has a carefully planned agenda for the funeral arrangements. He approaches the local clan and asks to purchase a particular parcel of land owned by a man named Efron. Efron offers to give Avraham the plot of land as a gift, free of charge, yet Avraham insists on paying for it. Eventually, a price is set; the sum is apparently exorbitant, especially considering the opening "price" offered by the seller.

While some Jews take pride in their business savvy, their forefather Avraham's negotiation skills seem to have been sorely lacking: He overpays for something he could have procured for free. To make matters even worse, Avraham had been promised this entire land as his inheritance. Why did he insist on paying for something that God Himself would eventually deliver to him on a silver platter?

Avraham had not "forgotten" that this land would eventually belong to him; in fact, God's promise was precisely the reason Avraham behaved so strangely in this negotiation. Part and parcel of God's promise that Avraham would inherit the Land of Israel was a "price" to be paid: "Know with certainty that your descendants will be strangers in a land that is not theirs and

Parashat Hayei Sarah

they will be enslaved and oppressed, for four hundred years"
(*Bereishit* 15:13).

The standard translation of this verse presents us with a
much-debated problem: The Jews were not enslaved in Egypt
for four hundred years. However, if the verse is read while
taking into account the cantillation symbols that also serve to
punctuate the Hebrew text, a very different parsing emerges:
"Know with certainty that your descendants will be strangers
in a land that is not theirs for four hundred years; [at times,]
they will be enslaved and oppressed." This nuanced reading of
the text is not always conveyed correctly in translation, but the
gist of the verse is that the four hundred years describes the
duration of time in which they would be strangers or foreigners,
devoid of sovereignty. The verse describes a period of time in
which Avraham's descendants would be a political minority in
the land that would eventually belong to them, and not a period
of four hundred years of oppression and enslavement.

Avraham had a very clear understanding of the promise
God had made to him; in fact, he made reference to it in his
negotiations with the locals: "I am a stranger [or 'foreigner']
and a resident among you," he said. "Allot for me a burial
place among you so that I can bury my dead" (*Bereishit* 23:4).
Avraham understood his political situation, and acknowledged
his current position as less-than-equal among the lords of
the land. He echoed God's use of the word *ger* to describe his
status as an outsider among the locals, indicating that despite
his absolute conviction that this land will eventually belong to
his descendants, he and his children, grandchildren and great-
grandchildren will continue to be "strangers" for four hundred
years—first in Canaan, then in the house of Lavan, and finally in

A Taste of Eden

Egypt. The local Canaanite population will continue to control politics, commerce, and the military until the full price for the Land of Israel is paid and God's promise comes to fruition.

And so, Avraham insists on paying for the burial plot. He insists on burying Sarah specifically in that spot because he cherishes the land. He appreciates its significance and holiness, and he wants to be a part of it. He wants to make an acquisition, to establish a foothold, in this very unique place. Although he is quite aware of the price he and his descendants will have to pay to inherit the Land of Israel, he wants to own some small part of it in his own lifetime. He knows that he will continue to be a stranger in the eyes of the surrounding population, but he also knows that this acquisition is the down payment on the land. This is the beginning of ownership of the Land of Israel which will last forever. Avraham did not want Efron to give it to him as a gift, for if it were "given" (and not sold) to him by anyone other than God, in the proper time, it would not really belong to him. Sarah's burial was, figuratively and literally, the act that planted the roots of the Jewish People in the Land of Israel— and Avraham would not allow this act to be based on the on-again-off-again largesse of the local Canaanite population.

Efron must have thought that he had hoodwinked Avraham, taking from him four hundred silver shekels for a burial plot, but Avraham was sure that he had made a wonderful deal. For a mere four hundred coins of silver, he had made the first acquisition in the Land of Israel, placing a down payment on the land that would be inherited by his descendants four hundred years later.

Parashat Toldot
Stand-up Comedy

"These are the generations of Yitzchak the
son of Avraham; Avraham fathered Yitzchak."
(*Bereishit* 25:19)

Readers of this *parashah*'s first verse cannot help but notice the
redundancy: If Yitzchak is the son of Avraham, there should
be no need to state that Avraham fathered Yitzchak. Rashi,
ever sensitive to the subtleties of language, tells us a back-story
which explains this strangely-worded verse.

Yitzchak's miraculous birth to a ninety-year-old mother
and a hundred-year-old father was fodder for the ancestors
of late night television's stand-up comics. In Rashi's words,
"The comedians of the generation claimed that Sarah became
pregnant from Avimelech..." (Rashi on *Bereishit* 25:19).

Apparently, even in Avraham and Sarah's day, cheap shots
were the stock in trade of clowns and cynics. The tabloids, as
it were, went for the cheap laugh, at the expense of Yitzchak—
as well as Avraham and Sarah. They preferred not to entertain
the possibility that these people lived a life of holiness, and that
they were blessed with a miracle. Instead, dirty minds let seedy
imaginings come up with an alternate version, offering a "more

rational" explanation for Yitzchak's birth. To these purveyors of gossip, destroying Avraham and Sarah's reputation was merely collateral damage.

But was the stand-up version of events any more plausible than the miraculous truth of Yitzchak's birth? For some reason, the cynics considered the pregnancy of a ninety-year-old woman who had suffered decades of infertility, to be rational, plausible, natural. What they refused to accept was the possibility that a man ten years her senior was capable of fathering a child. Such is the power of cynicism: It plants seeds of doubt even when the alternative narrative is equally implausible, or worse.

Rashi does not reveal the identity of these cynics, but a careful reading of the text in an earlier chapter will help us identify one of them, whose cynical and derisive laughter began as soon as Yitzchak was born.

> And Sarah saw the son of Hagar the Egyptian, whom she had borne to Avraham, laughing. And Sarah said to Avraham, "Banish this handmaid and her son, for the son of this handmaid shall not inherit with my son, with Yitzchak." (*Bereishit* 21:9-10)

At first glance, the reader might be taken aback by Sarah's reaction: Everything surrounding Yitzchak's life—even before his birth—is wrapped in joy and laughter. Avraham laughed when he was informed that Sarah would have a child; in fact, Sarah herself laughed. After Yitzchak was born, Sarah declared that all who hear her happy news will laugh with joy. Why, then, is Sarah incensed by Yishmael's laughter? Clearly, Sarah felt that Yishmael was not laughing out of joy, but smirking

Parashat Toldot

in derision. He was one of those cynics, one of the comedians who had a cheap laugh about the absurdity of Avraham having fathered Yitzchak.[2]

Upon consideration, this is bizarre: Why would Yishmael risk calling Avraham's ability to father a child into question? Would he himself not be tarred by the same brush, his own lineage called into question? Apparently, Yishmael was troubled by the birth of Avraham's new son—a son who would threaten Yishmael's birthright and status as Avraham's sole heir. Sarah is unfazed by Yishmael's cynicism; she sees right through his one-liners and goes straight to the heart of the matter, addressing Yishmael's underlying motives: "And Sarah said to Avraham, 'Banish this handmaid and her son, for the son of this handmaid shall not inherit with my son, with Yitzchak'" (*Bereishit* 21:10). Sarah does not voice criticism of Yishmael's behavior, nor does she make any effort to rebut Yishmael's slanderous barbs. She focuses on the question of inheritance, because that is what Yishmael is really after.

Yishmael's *modus operandi* is oddly familiar to us in its modern-day version: Jealousy and hatred of others that becomes so profound, so consuming, that a person becomes willing to suffer, even to die, in order to harm the object of their hatred. The suicide bomber is a direct descendant of the strange character found in this section of the Torah, the "suicide comic," who is willing to harm his own chances of inheritance as long as he harms the object of his jealousy and hatred in the process.

With this in mind, we may now return to our opening verse, that strangely redundant description of Yitzchak's

---

2. A number of commentaries connect the smirking of Yishmael with jesters and comedians. See Seforno and *Beit Yitzchak* on *Bereishit* 21:9; *Sefer Ma'aseh Hashem Chelek Ma'aseh Avot* Chapter 19.

A Taste of Eden

lineage: Indeed, Avraham fathered Yitzchak, and Yitzchak was the son of Avraham—a miraculous child, born to wonderful parents. Some people were overjoyed when they heard about this miracle. For others, it fueled laughter of a different sort: Smirking, knowing glances, and cynicism. With all the progress the world has made over the past four thousand years, things have not changed all that much.

Parashat Vayetzei
Feet on the Ground, Head in the Sky

Our *parashah* begins with Yaakov on the run; every aspect of his life is complicated. Although he leaves his hometown laden with blessings, at least some of these blessings were obtained under false pretenses. His relationships with each of the members of his family are clouded by these blessings, as is the journey on which he has embarked: Why is he going? Has he set out to find a bride, or is he a fugitive hoping to escape his brother's wrath? Is he heeding his father's wishes or his mother's advice?

How had things become so complicated? Yaakov's life had once been simple and straightforward; he had led a spiritual and cerebral existence, happily ensconced in the tent of study. How had things come so far? How had his situation become so impossible? His mother had instructed him to dupe his father; heeding her instructions would have been wrong, and disobeying her instructions would have been wrong. What choice did he have? And worse, how would this affect his relationship with God? Now that the deed was done, how would God react to these blessings and the way they were obtained? Would blessings attained in this manner have any potency or validity? Perhaps Yaakov could take solace in the fact that his departure for Paddan Aram was something both his parents agreed upon, albeit for different reasons.

In fact, Yitzchak and Rivka seemed to see their sons from totally different perspectives. Fortunately, readers of the text can pinpoint the crucial point of departure between these perspectives: Yitzchak saw his two sons as part of one family. His own early experience may have reinforced his desire to keep his sons together, united. Despite their different personalities, Yitzchak saw Yaakov and Esav as brothers, members of a single family and progenitors of one nation. It was his sincere hope that each of them would perfect their unique attributes, and together, as a united team, they would divide between them the responsibilities and capabilities that would bring God's blessing to fruition. Yaakov envisioned a partnership between the spiritual man of the tents and the powerful man of the fields.

Rivka's perspective was totally different. She saw her two sons as progenitors of two separate nations. Her insight was based upon "inside information":

God said to her, "Two nations are in your womb. Two governments will separate from inside you." (*Bereishit* 25:23)

Rivka understood that the personalities of her two sons were irreconcilable; these two nations would be in conflict, not in harmony. They would be working towards opposing goals, not as two halves of a united whole. This insight compelled her to push Yaakov into Yitzchak's room, to insure that her spiritual son would be given the blessings of physical and economic strength that would insure his survival.

Parashat Vayetzei

For his part, Yaakov much preferred to be a man of the tents, an occupation and outlook that surely conjured up memories and comparisons to his illustrious grandfather Avraham. On the other hand, Esav bore a striking similarity to Avraham's nemesis, the first "great hunter" — Nimrod. Yitzchak envisioned a partnership between these titans. If Yaakov and Esav could join forces, bringing together the great spiritual power of Avraham with the great political and military might of Nimrod, unparalleled greatness could be achieved. Rivka understood that this merger was not to be; both of these roles would have to fall on the shoulders of Yaakov alone.

Despite Yitzchak's great utopic dream, Rivka has clarity of vision and purpose. Yaakov obeys his mother and defers to the Divine insight she possesses; he steps up and accepts the dual role, despite his own proclivities and preferences. He understands that he must acquire both blessings—the physical, political and economic blessing that Yitzchak had intended to give to Esav, as well as the spiritual blessing—the promise God had made to Avraham which included inheriting the Land of Israel—that had always been intended for him. The question is—will God agree? Will He stand behind both of these blessings, or will the subterfuge involved in obtaining them invalidate one or both?

And if God does agree, how will Yaakov live up to this dual task? How will he reinvent himself? Can this man of the tents now become a man of the field? Can he live up to the challenges that these blessings will inevitably bring in their wake? How will Yaakov deal with the tension between the two opposing aspects of his life?

All of these questions are answered in the beginning of this *parashah*. God appears to Yaakov and assures him that the blessings given to Avraham will indeed come to fruition. Yaakov is the chosen one, and he will be the patriarch of a great nation that will inherit the Land of Israel.

The specific vision that Yaakov sees, of a ladder reaching from the ground up to the heavens, is particularly apt. With this image, Yaakov is able to process and assimilate the upheaval in his life, and to begin to forge his new reality. From the moment he leaves his father's home, Yaakov treads unfamiliar ground—the life of the man of the field. Yaakov understands that he will have to find a way to do what Esav would not: To create harmony between the physical, mundane life of the field and the spiritual life of the tents of study and prayer. The vision of the ladder is, at one and the same time, an expression of Yaakov's mission, and an expression of God's assurance that Yaakov is capable of fulfilling this mission—of creating a merger of these two opposites, the physical and the spiritual. This is the life to which Yaakov will aspire, and the imperative he bequeaths to each and every one of his descendants: His feet planted firmly on the ground, and his head reaching up to the heavens.

Parashat Vayishlach
Preparing for Battle, Praying for Peace

Years ago, as then-Prime Minister of Israel Menachem Begin prepared for a critical meeting with Presidents Sadat and Carter, he stopped in New York on the way to Washington. There he met individually with three of the great rabbis of that generation, Rabbis Moshe Feinstein, Menachem Schneerson, and Yosef Soloveitchik. From reports I have heard, all three rabbis gave Begin the same advice: Before the fateful meeting, review the Torah portion of *Vayishlach*.

This advice reflects the rabbinic understanding of the *parashah*, expressed in the midrash (*Bereishit Rabbah* 78:15) and reiterated in Ramban's commentary on the Torah (*Bereishit* 32:4), that the section dealing with the dramatic meeting between Yaakov and Esav was not just a "biblical story." Rather, it contains within it a prophetic program for future diplomatic, political, and even geo-political encounters that should be heeded throughout the long years of Jewish exile.

The context is Yaakov's impending return to Israel, the land of his birth, the land promised to him by his father and later by God Himself. Yaakov was now nearing the borders of his promised land, but there was a "catch"; for Yaakov, nothing ever happens the easy way. He had just escaped unscathed from a

A Taste of Eden

skirmish with his father-in-law Lavan, and was about to contend with the matter of his brother, who might still be piqued over certain blessings that had made their way to Yaakov.

Yaakov makes the first move. He sends a delegation to his brother Esav, bearing gifts and words of rapprochement. The response brought back by these messengers is ominous: Esav is on his way, with an "escort" of four hundred men. While Yaakov tries to avoid war with gifts, Esav seems poised for battle. Yaakov divides his household into two camps; he reasons that if one camp is attacked, the other might escape.

Our Sages extrapolate both economic and communal conclusions from Yaakov's preparations: One should not "put all of their eggs in one basket," or, in the words of the midrash, "Do not put all your money in one corner" (*Bereishit Rabbah* 76:3). This lesson is taken beyond the purely monetary realm, and the Rabbis stress that the same principle is true regarding even more valuable "commodities"—people. Just as Yaakov hoped to minimize the toll of war and to insure his family's survival in case of attack, so, too, should the Jewish People plan for the worst, and attempt to save even a portion of the dispersed and persecuted Jewish nation. If the Jews in one community are in danger, hopefully another community will survive; when, for example, the community in the "south" (presumably Israel) is under threat, steps must be taken to insure the survival of the Jewish community in the Diaspora. The sages of the midrash had seen the First and Second Temples destroyed, and they developed a pragmatic strategy for Jewish survival, a strategy that dated back to Yaakov: Divide and survive. In fact, the midrash itself tells us that this *parashah* was more than just the source of general wisdom; it served as required reading,

Parashat Vayishlach

as the text with which representatives of the besieged Jewish community prepared themselves for meetings with the ruling authorities.

A careful reading of this episode teaches us that Yaakov took a three-pronged approach to his precarious situation: First, he attempted to make peace, sending a conciliatory message and showering his brother with gifts. Yaakov also turned to God in a prayer for peace and deliverance from harm, while simultaneously taking practical defensive steps to minimize the damage in the event that the worst-case scenario would unfold. Indeed, this formula has been applied throughout thousands of years of Jewish history: Paying "tributes," taxes, and ransoms to the lords of the lands in which the Jews lived, dispersing Jewish enclaves to the farthest corners of the known world to insure that not all would be lost, and a great deal of prayer.

Rabbinic sources refer to this strategy specifically regarding Rome, the symbol of Christendom. We cannot help but wonder how Prime Minister Begin read this passage. Would our Sages have been more worried about dealing with President Carter than with President Sadat?

In recent history, our return to the Land of Israel in vast numbers has created a double-edged sword. On the one hand, more and more Jews are concentrated in a small, defined geographic area, which makes the threat to Jewish survival more acute. On the other hand, the Jewish People now has, for the first time in thousands of years, the ability to fight back, to protect itself against the constant threats of persecution, exile, and annihilation. This new/old reality has engendered a gradual paradigm shift, in which Yaakov's example, which was predominantly a Diaspora model (as observed by the

A Taste of Eden

Ramban on *Bereishit* 33:15), has become augmented by the example set by Yaakov's sons. Rather than pulling up stakes or avoiding conflict when their sister Dina was abused, they chose the opposite path. They were unwilling to defer to their adversaries, and stood up to claim their rights as equals, at the very least, among the community of nations. This inevitably led to confrontation—the type of confrontation Yaakov preferred to avoid.

Parashat Vayeshev
Reading the Signs

The situation quickly spiraled out of control: Words, dreams, jealousy, and hatred—and then, talk of murder. Yaakov's family had always been a complicated one, with children from different mothers creating a difficult dynamic, especially when there was a clear favorite: The "golden child," Yosef.

Yosef lorded it over his brothers. He was made to feel special, and in turn he earned his brothers' resentment by being judgmental and reporting their misdeeds to his father. But for Yaakov's other sons, the proverbial icing on the cake was Yosef's apparent need to tell them about his dreams, his delusions of grandeur, his fantasy that he would rule over the family. Yaakov, who never does seem to realize the depth of the hatred directed toward Yosef, unwittingly contributes to the situation and sends Yosef to look in on the other sons and report back. And so, when they see him approach, they conspire to murder their spoiled, arrogant brother—and prove once and for all that his dreams are in fact the stuff of fantasy.

We should recall that these same brothers had previously "solved" a problem by resorting to bloodshed against someone (and his entire city) who had abused their sister. It seems they had extrapolated some skewed conclusions from that episode, namely, that violence solves problems. When they felt "abused" by Yosef, they turned to the same solution they had used so successfully before: Violence and bloodshed. This time, the victim would be their own flesh and blood, their (half-)brother Yosef.

They strip Yosef of his regal clothing and throw him in a pit. But then something happens that dissuades them from following through with their heinous plan. Perhaps savoring their opportunity to torture the object of their jealousy, they sit down—within earshot of Yosef's screams and pleas for mercy—and eat a meal. Suddenly, they see something that they apparently interpret as a Divine message: A caravan of Yishmaelites, heading toward Egypt. There, right before their eyes, is the solution God has sent them, a solution both elegant and befitting their most revered family tradition: No lesser role model than their great-grandmother Sarah had solved the problems of discord in Avraham's tent by sending away the offending half-brother, Yishmael. Although Avraham was hesitant, God Himself intervened and instructed Avraham to acquiesce to his wife's wisdom and maternal insight. Mothers, after all, do know best—especially matriarchs.

To their minds, the same problem Sarah had faced was repeating itself, and the solution was literally staring them in the face. They saw the appearance of the Yishmaelites as a sign from heaven, as a message from Sarah herself. The message they heard was that they should send their problematic half-brother away with the Yishmaelite caravan, and the problem of Yosef (like the problem of Yishmael) would be solved once and for all.

If that sign was not strong enough, a second group of pretenders come by at the most fortuitous moment to reinforce the message, just in case the brothers missed it: A band of Midianites appears on the scene. They, too, are descendants of Avraham, children of a concubine Avraham had taken late in life. They, too, were sent away—by Avraham; they would not inherit the Land of Israel or the blessings given to Avraham. They, like the children of Yishmael, were the disenfranchised descendants of a common patriarch. Both Yishmael and Midian were discredited pretenders to the inheritance of Avraham.

As the brothers see the scene unfold before them, they are convinced that they are doing the right thing. Avraham and Sarah are clearly with them, and God has given them a dramatic sign to support their chosen course of action. They need not kill Yosef; God wants them to send him away, to reduce his stature to that of a slave, and to banish him along with the other pretenders to the legacy of Avraham.

Although the brothers were convinced of their own righteousness, there is an unavoidable problem with their interpretation of events: They misunderstood Yosef, misjudged his character and capabilities, and most importantly, misjudged God's estimation of Yosef. Yosef was never rejected by God. The brothers could easily have done a "reality check"; they could have sought out their father's opinion and guidance, or perhaps even turned to their grandfather Yitzchak, who apparently was still alive, and who knew a thing or two about family rifts. But deep down, they knew that Yaakov would side with Yosef, and Yitzchak would stop at nothing to prevent them from causing a split in the family and casting out their brother. The brothers had no desire to hear these opinions and would not have heeded advice or guidance that so sharply differed from what they wanted to hear. They preferred to seek out signs and messages

A Taste of Eden

that supported their bloodlust, signs that seemed to justify their behavior as they sinned against Yosef, against their father, and against God. Sometimes the worst sins are the ones perpetrated when the sinner thinks he or she is doing a mitzvah.

Even people who think of themselves as most sincere can see "signs" and discern messages that support their own view of the world, and tend to disregard or even actively avoid dissonant information. When pursuing their chosen path, people tend to interpret events in a selfish, self-serving fashion. In this case, the brothers could just as easily have interpreted the appearance of the Yishmaelite and Midianite caravans in the opposite manner. Had they made the effort to re-examine their own motives, they would have read these "signs" as a message of conciliation and repentance: Yosef, unlike Yishmael and Midian, was loved and cherished by his father. Whereas Sarah and Avraham saw that Yishmael and Midian had no place in the emerging Jewish Nation, Yaakov saw in Yosef what the brothers could not: Yosef was gifted, special, and would one day realize all of the dreams of his youth. He would, indeed, grow to spiritual and political greatness, and would become the backbone and savior of the entire family. The day would come when he would lead not only his brothers, but all of Egypt. His dreams would come to fruition: His brothers would bow to him and turn to him for economic support.

Rather than finding signs to support their jealousy, the brothers should have been able to read the signs that pointed to Yosef's unique personality, and then join together to strengthen their family and their future. Instead, they saw only what they wished to see.

Parashat Miketz
Staring at the Truth

After many years, they meet again. They had parted ways years ago, a parting that was the result of a unilateral decision taken by one side—the stronger side, the majority: The brothers of Yosef. Yosef had been unceremoniously cast aside, sold into slavery and apparently forgotten. A lifetime has passed; twenty-two years. How many times had Yosef thought of the words he would say to his brothers when they would meet again? Surely he had thought the scenario through. He knew, with near-certainty, that the moment would come, and here it was: Standing before him were people who were once his brothers. This came as no surprise to him, for Yosef had always excelled at long-term vision, analysis and planning; it was the short term, the here and now, which seems to have confounded him.

When he was young, he had told his brothers of his dreams, how their sheaves would bow to his. They thought it laughable, impossible, yet Yosef knew it would be so. They ridiculed his dreams and interpretations, and sold him as a slave. They would hear no more of his ludicrous predictions. They would have nothing more to do with him (or so they thought), and they would make certain that his dreams would never come true.

A Taste of Eden

Nine years earlier, Pharaoh had told Yosef his own dream, also centered around a vision of grain, and Yosef intuited that his dream and Pharaoh's dream would merge. And so it was. Once again, Yosef was dressed in royal clothing. Once again, he was put in charge, and once again he was lauded for displaying wisdom beyond his years. He saw the prosperous years coming, but he knew they would be followed by hard and dry years that would bring famine—and, eventually, his brothers. Yosef knew that they would have no choice but to come seeking food, and they would prostrate themselves before him, literally bowing to his sheaves of grain. But what would he say when they stood before him?

Perhaps over those long years, years punctuated by solitude, years of separation from his family, years as a slave and then a prisoner, Yosef had learned not to speak until spoken to. Servitude and slavery have a way of modifying one's behavior. So, he waited. What would his brothers say? This would be the moment he had waited for, a moment of vindication, and Yosef must have imagined every detail of the scene: They will walk in and bow before him, the second most powerful man in Egypt. When they respectfully raise their gaze, they will realize that the man who holds their lives in his hands, the man before whom they are kneeling in deference and supplication, is none other than Yosef. The brothers will no doubt search for the right words to say to him. Will they speak words of apology, as if an apology could undo what they had done to him? Will they speak words of complete capitulation, words filled with humility and embarrassment? Will they find the words to say that Yosef had been right all along, and they had been so very wrong—about him, about his dreams, and about themselves? As they stand

Parashat Miketz

before him, Yosef waits for these words of vindication, every fiber of his being straining to listen for the nuances of meaning in their words. He waits with baited breath for his brothers to lift their eyes and see him, truly see him, for who he is.

But something goes terribly wrong. When the brothers do lift their eyes, they do not see their long-lost brother. They see a menacing Egyptian viceroy, a dangerous man with the power to decide their fate. There is no glimmer of recognition in their eyes, no quizzical look on their faces, as if the man before them is somehow familiar to them from a different time or place that they cannot quite recall. They do not speak; no words of reconciliation are uttered. There is nothing between them. They bow, as protocol dictates, and then rise before the powerful Egyptian ruler. If this was the moment Yosef had been waiting for, it proved to be tremendously anticlimactic and completely unsatisfactory—or even worse.

Years earlier, when the brothers had sold Yosef, they had denied his dreams and denied his greatness. Now, they denied his very existence. In a sense, their failure to recognize him may have been worse than the sale itself. Years earlier, they denied the dreams as a possibility; now, as the (first) dream comes to fruition, the brothers seem oblivious to the magnitude of what is happening. When they say nothing, Yosef understands the sad truth: For his brothers, the dreams were not prophetic; they were, and still are, fantasy. In their minds Yosef had always been, and would always be, a slave. In their minds, they had done the right thing by selling him into slavery, for they had merely "returned" him to his rightful station. His brothers have no words for him—not a word of reconciliation, regret or even any words with which to explain their behavior, only silence.

A Taste of Eden

They have come for food, and nothing more. They treat him like a stranger.

Yosef returns the strangeness and estrangement with his distant, aloof tone. On the other hand, he asks personal questions about their family: Where are they from? How many siblings are they? Is their father well? A strange dance begins, in which only one side hears the music, only one side knows the choreography, only one side moves with any semblance of logic. From the brothers' perspective, Yosef is perplexing, strange, and mysterious. They do not anticipate any of his moves, do not understand what he is doing, fail to see what he wants, and most importantly, they never guess his identity. And therein lies the rub: Why are they never able to deduce the identity of their tormentor?

The brothers were so entrenched in their world-view, a view that saw Yosef as an inferior, that they were unable to recognize him—even when he stood right in front of them and asked about their father and their long-lost brother. Such is the nature of hatred: It causes you to devalue the object of your hatred, even in the face of all evidence to the contrary. The brothers could not see Yosef; their hatred and jealousy blinded them to his true value. In their eyes, he was but a slave and would never amount to anything more than that. When Yosef actually stands before them in his royal garb, wielding unsurpassed power and influence, when they come face to face with the man revered and respected by all of Egypt, when they themselves bow to him and watch his dreams comes true, they are incapable of recognition.

Hatred causes blindness. A cold, logical analysis should have brought the brothers to the obvious conclusion that the only person who would care so much about their family, who would ask to see Binyamin, who would express concern for their father's health, was Yosef. But the brothers were so blinded by their hatred that they could not see the truth staring right at them. And that is the real tragedy of Yosef's life.

Parashat Vayigash
Becoming Yehuda

Eleven sons of Yaakov stand, accused and threatened, before one of the most powerful men in the world, second in command in a regime not known for compassion or forgiveness. They must make a decision, and their options, though seemingly straightforward, are actually quite complex.

Once again, a son of Rachel has apparently behaved in an unseemly fashion. When Binyamin is caught with the cup of the powerful leader in his bag, the brothers are faced with several possible choices. Self-preservation would dictate that they part ways with their brother Binyamin just as they did with Yosef years ago; however, their present situation seems much more complicated. The only reason Binyamin has joined them in Egypt is to serve as proof that they are, in fact, brothers, and not spies. Like true brothers, they could close ranks and follow Binyamin wherever fate takes him, be it incarceration or even death, and demand that they all be treated as one family, sharing the same fate. Perhaps this moral stance would help them assuage their own consciences, though it would most likely not achieve any other desirable results. Should they gamble that opting to share in Binyamin's punishment will convince their

Parashat Vayigash

Egyptian tormentor that they have been speaking the truth, that they are, in fact, brothers, and that they should all be set free?

What if they choose the opposite path, the option being offered to them by the Egyptian justice system, and simply walk away, washing their hands of their brother, the last remaining favored son of the favored wife? If they accept the offer, cut their losses, and leave Binyamin behind, will they fail the test they are being put through, thus sealing their own doom as well as Binyamin's? Is this a test, a trap, or a straightforward execution of Egyptian justice?

Faced with this quagmire, Yehuda suggests a third solution—a solution that seems, given his personal track record, completely uncharacteristic and unexpected. Yehuda suggests that he and Binyamin change places: Binyamin will go home to his father, while Yehuda will face a life of servitude.

Yehuda's first "speaking role" in the Torah is in the scene on the outskirts of Dotan, in the Land of Israel. Yosef has been stripped of his special coat and thrown into a pit, and the brothers table two possibilities: Murder Yosef in cold blood, or leave him in the pit to die as nature takes its course. For the first time, Yehuda speaks; apparently, he is so charismatic that all the alternative plans suggested by his brothers are quickly abandoned, and his plan embraced: In his first known attempt at leadership, Yehuda proposes that they sell their brother into slavery rather than killing him. Yehuda speaks and his brothers listen.

This solution is both cunning and self-serving: Not nearly as messy as murder, neither in a literal nor emotional sense, Yehuda's plan manages to "remove" Yosef without bloodshed while turning a handsome profit. In one fell swoop, the "Yosef Problem" is solved and Yehuda is established as leader of the brothers. There is no expression or even intimation of concern for his father or for Yosef.

The chapter immediately following the sale of Yosef reinforces what we have already seen of Yehuda's character: He is charismatic, self-absorbed, self-involved, and gives no thought whatsoever to his daughter-in-law Tamar's needs or feelings. We might be tempted to describe him as a borderline narcissistic personality, for whom the concept of "empathy," if it exists in his lexicon at all, is something others should have for him, and not vice versa.

And yet, as he stands before this strange and menacing Egyptian prince, a different Yehuda emerges. Something, or someone, has transformed him from the narcissistic young man he once was into a person who considers others' needs before his own. To be sure, years have passed and the tragedy of losing two of his own sons has had some impact, but there is something more to his metamorphosis. Yehuda goes far beyond what we would expect from an empathetic person. He does not merely beg for mercy on his brother Binyamin's behalf. He is willing—wholeheartedly and immediately—to sacrifice himself in order to save Binyamin, in order to spare his father any more pain, in order to fulfill the promise he made to Yaakov. He takes a leadership role, but more importantly, he takes responsibility.

How did this change come about? Simply stated, Yehuda had a very good teacher. The person who changed him, who taught him self-sacrifice, was an elegant woman with an extreme sense of morality and justice: His daughter-in-law, Tamar. Yehuda had abandoned Tamar, in effect sentencing her to a life in limbo as a "living widow." Tamar took her fate into her own hands, and seduced the willing Yehuda by pretending to be a prostitute. However, when she stood accused of adultery, she chose the moral high ground. Rather than publicly exposing Yehuda's hypocrisy and taking him to task for his selfish disregard of his legal and moral obligations, she decided not to embarrass him or to seek revenge. As she was led to her own execution, she sent a cryptic message that hinted at the identity of her paramour—a message that only Yehuda could decipher. And then, something magical happened: The self-absorbed borderline-narcissist developed a conscience, and admitted his guilt. What happened? Why did Yehuda make this dramatic admission when no one would ever know the damning truth?

Tamar's self-sacrifice taught Yehuda a powerful lesson and transformed him from selfish to selfless. Now, as Yehuda unknowingly stands before his estranged brother, he rejects the two options that are on the table. He will neither abandon his brother and sentence him to a life of slavery, as he himself had once advocated, nor will he make the futile gesture of joining Binyamin in servitude. He makes an unexpected third choice, offering himself in Binyamin's stead: His youngest brother must be returned to their father. Yehuda has learned and internalized the lessons he learned from Tamar: self-sacrifice, empathy, responsibility—and love.

The contrast between this scene and the scene at the mouth of the pit in Dotan is unmistakable. Yehuda is still a leader, but he now displays a different type of leadership. The qualities he has learned, the qualities he will bequeath to his descendants, are the defining qualities of true Jewish leadership, from David through the Messiah: self-sacrifice, empathy and an immutable moral compass. Yehuda places the needs of others before his own. This sort of leadership was, and always will be, the catalyst for the salvation of the Jewish People.

Parashat Vay'chi
Take Me Home

As Yaakov nears the end of his life, he summons his son Yosef and pleads with him to see to it that he is given a proper burial in the land of Canaan. We are unsure why it is specifically Yosef whom he entrusts with this task: Perhaps only Yosef, of all the sons of Yaakov, has the power to fulfill this request. Alternatively, this may indicate that Yaakov still favors Yosef above his other sons: It is Yosef that he trusts and, Yaakov believes, Yosef who will return his love and tend to him, even after his passing.

Had the special relationship between Yaakov and Yosef been rekindled after the long years of separation? Had father and son simply picked up where they left off before their lives were so rudely interrupted, or had the events that preceded their reunion served to make their relationship even closer? After all, the violence that brought Yosef to Egypt, the years of estrangement, loneliness and abuse Yosef suffered, as well as his eventual success, all mirrored Yaakov's own biography. Could father and son have become even more alike as the years went by?

Perhaps, instead, Yosef had been changed by his experiences, and Yaakov turned to him now as a subject pleading with a powerful foreign ruler. Had the years in Egypt or the nearly-unlimited power he now enjoyed corrupted him, or was Yosef still the most loyal son of Yaakov, the most eager to please and obey his father, the great protégé of Yaakov?

Externally, Yosef had certainly undergone a transformation. Ever since he was brought before Pharaoh, he dressed as an Egyptian. His trappings and manner did not belie his origins as a young Hebrew slave. He wore the robes of Egyptian royalty, as did his wife and sons.

When Yosef stands before his father to receive Yaakov's blessing for his children, Yaakov does not seem to recognize his grandchildren. Perhaps Yaakov's advanced years and failing eyesight are to blame; perhaps the clouded vision is caused by a disturbing prophetic insight to which Yaakov is privy, regarding the descendants of Menashe and Efraim. The most straightforward explanation, though, is that these Egyptian princes seem quite strange to him.

Nonetheless, the blessing Yaakov gives them is telling: Menashe and Efraim are to be considered like Reuven and Shimon. First and foremost, this indicates that Yosef is being treated as the firstborn; he alone receives a double portion in the family's most prized inheritance. On the other hand, this blessing indicates that despite the years that separate Yosef's sons from the sons of Yaakov, despite the physical distance from their ancestral homeland and from their saintly grandfather, despite having been raised in the morally corrupt Land of Egypt, Yosef's children are no different than any of the sons of Yaakov. There is no generation gap. And this, more than anything else, reflects Yosef's greatness. Despite their strange garb, their fidelity to the vision of Avraham was intact.

Later, as Yosef's life comes to an end, he makes his extended family swear that they will take his remains with them when

A Taste of Eden

they leave Egypt. Yosef believed that the Children of Israel were not staying in Egypt. He was not confused by his own political or economic security. His identity was perfectly clear to him; his place was with the Children of Israel, in the Promised Land, and not in the pantheon of Egyptian leaders. For Yosef there would be no burial pyramid; no slaves and treasures would accompany him to the Egyptian afterlife. Perhaps in this final act, more than any other, we obtain a glimpse into Yosef's inner world.

Yosef knew that this Egyptian sojourn was a "temporary gig." He had no illusions about the vicissitudes of fate. He had seen high-ranking officials arrested, some quite suddenly plucked from death row and returned to office and others put to death. He himself went from prince to prisoner to slave and back again, only to find himself as the second most powerful man in the ancient world. He was far too wise to believe that it would, or should, last.

Yosef had acute long-term vision; he knew that God's control over the world is as direct and immediate on the national scale as it is on the personal scale. The Egyptian people, who had enjoyed years of plenty, suddenly found themselves as indentured servants to Pharaoh, in a policy Yosef himself had orchestrated. Who better than Yosef knew that such a reversal of fortunes could happen to his own people, that the shift from protected wards of the state to downtrodden slaves could and would happen, in no more than the blink of an eye? And, Yosef knew, just as suddenly the day would come when the Children of Israel would leave this place and head home, to the land promised to their forefathers.

That future, that destiny—and not the riches of an Egyptian tomb—were the stuff of Yosef's dreams and aspirations. Yosef's

Parashat Vay'chi

last request was that he be a part of the great march toward the destiny he shared with his people—his *real* people, his brothers. Although his allegiance may have been questioned during his lifetime, in death Yosef left no room for doubt. Beneath the Egyptian finery, he remained Yosef, the son of Yaakov. He was a Jew, and he wanted to go home.

Parashat Shemot
Redemption Song

Very suddenly, the servitude that had been predicted so many years earlier, in the covenant forged between God and Avraham beneath the dark and ominous evening sky, had come to fruition—but with an unforeseen twist: The Egyptian slave-masters began to imagine that their Israelite slaves were subhuman and had no rights whatsoever—not even the right to exist. A "final solution" had been set in motion. All the male children would be put to death and the females would be used as slaves of the most sordid kind, bringing an abrupt end to the family of Avraham before the second half of the covenant, redemption, could become a reality.

The genocidal program was in full swing, but before very long heroes emerged, brave women who refused to be a part of the Egyptian killing machine. These women defied the powerful Pharaoh and feared only the unseen, all-powerful God of their faith.

A close and careful reading of the first two chapters of the Book of *Shemot* reveals that it is the women who lead. Midwives and mothers, Moshe's sister Miriam and the daughter of Pharaoh: An overwhelming percentage of this story's protagonists are women. While the men slave away in the dismal present tense,

Parashat Shemot

the women insure the continuity of the Jewish People. With an acute sense of their past, they look toward the future and the great destiny they know awaits.

This preponderance of female figures was not lost on the sages of later generations, who articulated a foundational principle that has both philosophical and, quite possibly, halachic ramifications: "The redemption from Egypt was in the merit of righteous women."

In fact, there is one more woman who played a particularly important role in the redemption. Despite the fact that her name is not mentioned in these chapters, Serach, the daughter of Asher, was a pivotal figure in the crucial moments of Israelite history. When Moshe was finally cajoled into leading the people, he traveled to Egypt and stood before the elders of the nascent Jewish nation. Moshe showed them the signs and wonders with which God had equipped him, but the elders were unsure what to make of this talented stranger. They sought the counsel of an elderly woman, Serach, the daughter of Asher. They described the signs and wonders Moshe had performed for them, but Serach was unimpressed; Egypt was rife with magicians. Then, they repeated to her a particular phrase Moshe had used: "God has 'remembered' [*pakad*] the Children of Israel."[3] Immediately, Serach knew that Moshe was the chosen one, that he was, indeed, sent by God to lead them out of slavery and back to their homeland. Serach had been entrusted by her father with a tradition that was passed down by Avraham to Yitzchak, who passed it to Yaakov, who passed it on to Yosef, who, in turn, passed it on to his brothers, including her father Asher—a tradition regarding the precise words with which the

3. *Shemot* 4:31.

67

redemption would begin. As soon as she heard that Moshe had used this phrase, she knew that the time had come. The elders' doubts were immediately erased; Serach's decision was all that was needed to set in motion a chain of events that would change the world. [4]

The subsequent chapters are full of wonder and fury; eventually, the great moment arrived, and the Israelites were freed. They spent their last hours in Egypt amassing the spoils of their erstwhile oppressors, in fulfillment of God's promise to Avraham that they would leave with great wealth. However, one man was in pursuit of a different treasure. He, too, sought to fulfill a promise, but of a different sort: Moshe spent his last moments in the land of his birth seeking out the remains of Yosef, in order to fulfill the promise that had been made not to leave him behind when the redemption came. Moshe, too, had been a prince of Egypt, only to rejoin his brothers later in life, and he was determined to fulfill Yosef's dying wish—to return to his homeland.

But when Moshe was unable to locate Yosef's remains, he sought out the authoritative source of information. There was only one person, a vestige of the previous generations, who knew exactly where to find Yosef's remains: Serach, the daughter of Asher,[5] the keeper of secrets, the repository of tradition, the bridge across the generations.

What was it about Serach, more than anyone else, that prepared her for this role? There is a rabbinic teaching that traces Serach's unique talents back to a touching scene that

---

4. *Yalkut Shimoni: Lech Lecha Remez* 64.
5. Tosefta *Sotah* 4:7.

had transpired years before:[6] When the brothers returned from Egypt with the shocking news that Yosef was still alive, no one knew how to break this news to their elderly, fragile father Yaakov. They decide to entrust Yaakov's granddaughter, a young girl named Serach, with the delicate task—and with good reason.

While Yaakov stood in prayer, Serach sang to him: "Can it be so? Is Yosef truly in Egypt? This and more: Children were born to him, Menashe and Efraim!"

Serach knew the words that would liberate Yaakov from his pain and suffering, and she had the sensitivity to deliver the message in a way that her frail and bereft grandfather could accept. Similarly, years later, it was Serach who showed Moshe how to liberate Yosef from the depths of the Nile, just as she alone knew the words and tune that would liberate the entire people from their slavery. As she grew into adulthood and then into old age, she never forgot the tune she had sung to her grandfather. She retained that sensitivity and kept her ear attuned to the melody that was the key to Yaakov's personal liberation. As an adult, she taught that same song of freedom to Yaakov's descendants. Through it, they, too, knew that the redemption that had been promised so long ago would soon be a reality. From Serach, they—and we—learned the song of redemption.

---

6. *Midrash HaGadol*, cited in *Torah Shleimah* page 863 section 88 and note 88.

Parashat Va'era
Lessons in Leadership

As we endure yet another election season, leaders and leadership are on our minds—as they have been since the birth of our nation.

Of all the leaders the Jewish People has enjoyed or endured, Moshe was one of the greatest, and one of the most reluctant. From the outset, Moshe doubted both his suitability and his ability to speak for the people, or to the people. Words did not come easily to him. What sort of leader would he be without eloquence and elocution? God had to cajole and practically plead with Moshe, and to appoint his brother Aharon as his assistant, to convince Moshe to accept the job. Even so, Moshe continued to question his own leadership, and occasionally tried to return his mandate.

As the story of the exodus unfolds, we might wonder if Moshe actually had "the right stuff" for the job: As he feared, upon arriving in Egypt, the Israelites rejected him, and Moshe questioned how he would manage to sway Pharaoh if he was unable to convince even the Israelites (6:12). Perhaps Aharon, the older brother, the man who spoke the language of the people and to whom they turned for counsel and comfort, would have been a better choice? Apparently not: When push finally came to shove and Aharon was forced to take the reins in Moshe's absence—the result was the Golden Calf. Aharon had charisma, eloquence and the common touch, but he could not stare down an angry mob.

There is, however, a third leadership model to be found in this week's Torah portion; mentioned in passing, it slips by almost unnoticed. In the midst of Moshe's repeated attempts to demur (6:12, 6:30) we find a short, select genealogy of those destined to leave Egypt, culminating in Aharon's nuclear family. This genealogy is intended to establish Aharon's credentials, but the list is not what we would have expected. Describing Aharon's family, a unique formulation is used: Not only is Aharon's wife Elisheva mentioned, which is somewhat out of the ordinary, but so is her father, and, most unusual of all, her brother:

> Aharon married Nachshon's sister, Elisheva daughter
> of Aminadav. She bore him Nadav, Avihu, Elazar and
> Itamar. (6:23)

Noting this anomalous formulation, Rashi explains that Elisheva's brother Nachshon is included in order to teach us a life lesson: When choosing a spouse, bear in mind that the children will inherit personality traits from their mother's brothers.

What do we know about Elisheva's brother Nachshon? He, too, was a leader, but his leadership differed from that of Moshe or Aharon: While Moshe was reticent, Nachshon was a descendant of the charismatic Yehuda, known for being direct, even impetuous. While Aharon led with words, Nachshon led with deeds: He was the first of the tribal leaders to bring an offering the day the Tabernacle was consecrated, because, the Midrash tells us, he had been the first to leap into the sea. Pursued by the Egyptians, with their backs to the water, Nachshon was the first to take a leap of faith, leading the Israelites into the Red Sea before it split to clear a pathway for their escape (*Bemidbar Rabbah* 13:7). Nachshon is the prototype for commanders who lead by example, jump first into the fray and cry, *aharai!* – "Follow me!"

For his bravery and faith, for leading by example, Nachshon was rewarded the day the Tabernacle was consecrated. Once again, he was first.

But something else happened on that day: Two of Aharon's sons were consumed by a heavenly fire. Without waiting for instructions or permission, they brought an unsanctioned offering. When viewed through the prism of Rashi's haunting comments, we begin to see their impetuous behavior from a new perspective: They had, indeed, inherited their uncle Nachshon's personality traits, but unlike him, they had misused their gifts. To be sure, there is a time and a place for this type of leadership, but Nadav and Avihu were led astray by this same impetuousness, and were consumed by their own desire to blaze new trails. On the very same day Nachshon was rewarded, his impressionable nephews followed his example, leaping forward—with disastrous results.

This, then, is the third model of leadership in *Parashat Vaera*: Nachshon was charismatic, idealistic, strong and brave, but lacked self-restraint. His style of leadership was exciting, energizing—and somewhat dangerous. Aharon was eloquent and popular, but he was also non-confrontational, and lacked the strength to lead. In the final analysis, Moshe's hesitation and

Parashat Va'era

humility make him more attractive as a leader. He was never interested in the spotlight or the trappings of leadership; he assumed the role thrust upon him out of a sense of responsibility. He was convinced, after some effort on God's part, that no one else could get the job done. Moshe made up in competence what he lacked in charisma.

This essay originally appeared in The Jerusalem Report, *January 26, 2015.*

Parashat Bo
It's the Children

The plagues continue; in fact, their severity seems to have increased. Pounded by plague after plague, the Egyptians suffer both physical discomfort and financial ruin. Although the Israelites had, for generations, been the engine that powered the Egyptian economy, the price the Egyptians were now paying to keep the slaves had become excessive. Did Pharaoh not have a competent actuary capable of charting the financial folly of his policy of intransigence, or was he motivated by other concerns? Perhaps the slave-based economy and standard of living was not at the head of Pharaoh's list of problems; rather, his struggle to retain power and stature took precedence. Should Pharaoh capitulate to the demands of the lowest echelon of his kingdom, his days as ruler would be over. Things had already begun unraveling: Even his court advisers had become emboldened enough to do what had once been unthinkable: They voiced an opinion that contradicted Pharaoh's decision, advocating the freeing of the slaves. In their words, "Egypt is already lost" (*Shemot* 10:7).

Pharaoh, while steadfast in his refusal, begins to show some signs of weakening. In a step toward negotiating a partial and temporary release of the slaves, he inquires about the planned

74

Parashat Bo

three-day prayer retreat. Who will be going? (*Shemot* 10:8) Moshe responds that young and old, males and females— every single member of the Israelite nation, must be released. Pharaoh warns Moshe of the folly of this plan: It would be a terrible mistake, he tells him, to take everyone. To Pharaoh's mind, a religious experience of this sort is exclusively "men's work"; the women and children should be left behind. This may have been no more than self-serving advice, designed to insure that the slaves would not run off; alternatively, this may have been an expression of sincere concern, a moment of weakness on Pharaoh's part that allows us a glimpse of his inner world. Pharaoh warned Moshe not to make the mistake of creating a democratic society, a society lacking the clear caste distinctions on which Egyptian culture was based. To do so would be even more destabilizing than the plagues, as it would have a devastating domino effect on the very underpinnings of Pharaoh's rule. If men and women, boys and girls, young and old, people of all social strata, were to serve God equally in the wilderness, where would such feelings of equality lead?

This, of course, was a "deal breaker": Moshe would not agree to a partial exodus. Until they could all leave Egypt to serve God, they would not leave at all.

Had Pharaoh acquiesced, had he let them take a three-day furlough to serve God in the wilderness, the story would surely have had a different ending. The Egyptians' suffering and eventual death could have been averted; all Pharaoh had to do was to allow the Israelites universal worship. After this three-day religious experience, the Israelites would have returned to Egypt, to share the lessons they had learned with their erstwhile oppressors. Slavery and tyranny would have come to an end, and the Israelites would have marched on to the Promised Land.[7] The three days of universal worship in the wilderness would have endowed them, as a nation, with the spiritual fortitude to face whatever lay ahead; everyone, without exception, was to participate.

Moshe's demand stands in stark contrast to the longstanding Egyptian ethos. Egyptian society was built on a clearly defined hierarchy, not only between the sexes but in terms of utility: taskmasters, overseers, Israelite slave handlers, common slaves. From the outset, the Pharaohs had distinguished between men and women, boys and girls: The boys were to be killed, and the girls were to become personal slaves to the Egyptians. Moshe, on the other hand, lays out the first steps of the nascent Jewish nation, and his focus is not limited to the men or even to the adults. When Moshe makes this declaration of universal worship, an authentic Jewish ethic is born: Judaism's greatest investment is in the children. The Jewish People does not exist without the children, and we are willing to remain in Egypt as long as necessary, until such time as the children are freed. We will sacrifice for our children.

Tragically, Pharaoh chose the opposite track, preferring to sacrifice Egypt's children—even his own flesh and blood—to maintain the status quo. From the outset, Pharaoh had been warned that if the Jews (and their children) are not freed—the Egyptians' children will die. After nine plagues, it should have been clear to Pharaoh that Moshe's warnings were not empty threats, they were guarantees: The worst plague of all, the plague of the firstborn, was imminent.

---

7. I heard from Rabbi Soloveitchik make this point on numerous occasions.

Parashat Bo

The events recounted in this *parashah* teach us that our children were not merely a part of the Exodus story, they are the focus of the Exodus itself, and of the retelling of the tale every year on Passover Eve. For at least one night, every Jewish parent becomes a teacher and every Jewish child a student. Our children are the focus of the Passover Seder, and it is our duty to make them feel that they are a part of the events of the Exodus.

The education of our children is no academic exercise; it is a defining element of our religious identity. Although the Seder is a once-a-year lesson designed to draw our children into the Jewish experience, the investment we make in our children goes far beyond that one special night. It is a constant in Judaism that began with Moshe's declaration that everyone—men, women, and most importantly, children—worships God equally and directly. When we retell the Passover story each year at the Seder table, our children are the focus, just as they were the focus of the Exodus itself.

Parashat B'Shalach
Winds of Salvation

The moment they had dreamed of for hundreds of years had finally arrived: The Children of Israel were no longer slaves. They had been released from their bondage through a series of miracles, and were now taking their first steps as free people. Suddenly, they were faced with a threat for which they were ill-prepared: The mighty Egyptian army, equipped with state-of-the-art chariots and highly trained warriors, was bearing down on them. The Israelites took up whatever primitive arms they could in order to defend themselves and their new freedom, but they soon realized that their weapons and military capabilities were no match for their erstwhile oppressors. The fledgling nation and their rag-tag defense force found themselves between Scylla and Charybdis, trapped between the approaching Egyptian onslaught and the foreboding sea. It appeared the experiment of an independent Israelite nation would be exceedingly short-lived.

As their tension and fear rose to a fever-pitch, another miraculous intervention transpired: A strong easterly wind blew throughout the night, creating a passage of dry land in the sea through which the Israelites made their way without even getting their feet wet.

Parashat B'Shalach

In fact, the method behind this miraculous event might have appeared to be a natural phenomenon:

And Moshe stretched out his hand over the sea; and God caused the sea to recede by a strong east wind all that night, and turned the sea into dry land; and the waters were divided. (14:21)

Apparently, the Egyptian army—horses, chariots and all—were lulled into a false sense of security.[8] They saw what appeared to be a fortuitous juxtaposition of naturally occurring events, and proceeded into the passageway in pursuit of their fleeing slaves. And then, a miracle of unmistakable and enormous magnitude occurred: The waters seemed to "take sides" in this battle. The Egyptians became, quite literally, the victims of a sea change, as the waters returned to their place—with a vengeance.

Apparently, the salvation of the Jews was carried out by a miracle concealed in a natural phenomenon, while the eradication of the Egyptians was carried out by the unmistakable Hand of God, through the upending of the laws of nature. The blatantly, inescapably miraculous element of this chain of events was not the method through which the Israelites were saved, but the singular method through which the Egyptians received their much-deserved punishment.

Was this merely a question of strategy, a ruse to lure the unsuspecting Egyptians into the sea? Perhaps. However, rabbinic sources offer a different perspective. The Talmud reports that a heated debate was carried out in heaven regarding the justification for saving the Israelites. It was argued that both

8. See commentary of Ramban, *Shemot* 14:21.

the Jews and the Egyptians were deserving of death; in the words of one rabbinic teaching, "These are idolaters and these are idolaters." This may explain why the miraculous salvation of the Jews was subdued, and made to appear to be a natural event.

Interestingly enough, when we look back at the events, especially on Passover night as we read the Haggadah, we emphasize the miraculous splitting of the sea, and avert our focus from the punishment of the Egyptians. This is not simply political correctness; a very central element of the Seder is the message that we must focus on our salvation, and give thanks and praise to God for the miracles He performed for our benefit—even those that were disguised as natural phenomena. Just as Jews are acutely aware of the importance of timing for a good joke (always deliver the punchline just before people laugh), so, too, the timing of "natural phenomena" is what makes them miraculous. On that day, at the banks of the Red Sea, the timing of that east wind was Divine. The waters split just as the Israelites needed an escape route, and they came crashing back down as the Egyptians followed them into the sea. While the second part of the miracle may have been more conspicuous, may have left a greater impression of sound and fury, both the "natural" splitting of the sea and the "unnatural" closure of the safe passageway were miracles. In both cases, God took an active role in human history, but He chose different volume settings, as it were, to bring about these two miracles.

Perhaps this is the lesson of the Splitting of the Sea: Sometimes, miracles occur on a grand scale. Divine intervention is obvious, and only those with the most jaundiced eye can argue away the miracle. Other times, the Hand of God pulls strings behind the scenes, manipulating the natural course of events more subtly. How many times in our history has that "east wind" come to our rescue, perhaps unnoticed but, in retrospect, unmistakable? How many times throughout our history have we felt that same wind on our backs, almost imperceptibly steering us on the path to salvation? Can we, almost 50 years later, deny that the miraculous "east wind" of God's protection gusted for six days in June 1967? Then, and during so many other perilous junctures in Jewish history in which the very existence of the Jewish People was threatened, the miracles that saved our homeland and our People were often perceived as natural events. During the throes of a terrible storm, we may be unable to discern the benevolent gust of wind that brings salvation in its wake.

On Seder night, as we look back, we have the perspective and the insight born of distance and experience, and we recount the miracle of our salvation—a miracle compounded by many smaller, almost imperceptible miracles: Were there fifty, or two hundred, or even two hundred and fifty miracles at the Red Sea which brought about our salvation? This, then, is the way a Jew should learn history. Through this prism, we should consider world events as they unfold: The Hand of God is at work in the background, protecting and guiding us as a nation.

This lesson goes far beyond Passover Eve: God's involvement is not limited to the great historic upheavals or the struggles and triumphs of our nation. He is equally involved, in both conspicuous and inconspicuous ways, in the private life of each and every one of us. The Talmud stresses this with a well-known and touching lesson regarding the most personal aspect of our lives: God Himself is the ultimate matchmaker, and his efforts in this sphere are compared to the splitting of the Red

A Taste of Eden

Sea (*Sotah* 2a). Apparently, the analogy points out the subtle, seemingly-natural course of events that God sets in motion, that "east wind" that changes our lives and brings about our salvation.

Do we take the time to notice the Hand of God in our lives? Perhaps the Talmud's message is that our response should be the same as that of the Israelites at the Red Sea: When they finally grasped the magnitude of the "natural" miracles that had brought about their redemption, they broke into song and dance, and declared, "This is my God, and I will glorify Him!"

Parashat Yitro
Unity, not Uniformity

When the Jews arrived at Mount Sinai they were, in a very real sense, a brand new People. They had come down to Egypt as a family, perhaps even a tribe; now they were an emancipated nation. In a very short period of time they experienced a staggering series of national crises: The threat of war against a superpower, miraculous salvation and the celebration at the sea, as well as a surprise military attack at the hands of Amalek. They had seen miracles and experienced panic, but now, at the foot of Mount Sinai, they experienced something new: Unity.

The Torah's description of the Israelite encampment at Sinai includes a nuanced turn of phrase which is lost in the English translation. Whereas all of their travels and encampments up to this point are described in the plural, this stop alone is described in the singular:

In the third month after the Israelites left [plural] Egypt, on the first of the month, they [plural] came to the desert of Sinai. They [plural] had departed from Rephidim and had arrived [plural] in the Sinai Desert, camping (plural) in the wilderness. Israel camped [singular] opposite the mountain. (19:1-2)

A Taste of Eden

This unusual shift leads Rashi to describe the atmosphere of this particular encampment "as one person, with one heart." The rapturous description of a people in sync, connected, with one heartbeat, is one of the most uplifting messages in the entire Torah.

There is, however, a downside to unity: Too often, it is achieved through uniformity—particularly uniformity achieved by force. Individuals who don't "fit in" may feel threatened and lost. Moreover, uniformity can seep into the realm of ideas, stifling creativity and vanquishing individuality.

With these pitfalls in mind, a number of commentaries point out that the unity at the foot of Mount Sinai was the backdrop for the great Revelation, which itself was characterized by individuality: The theophany at Sinai was perceived, understood and appreciated by each and every member of the nation in a unique way. Each person experienced the Revelation in accordance with their unique personality, aptitude and capabilities. Rambam (Maimonides) succinctly expressed this school of thought[9] by explaining that what was revealed at Sinai was truth—absolute, pristine truth. Each person was able to perceive this truth according to their individual level of spiritual sensitivity.

The mystical tradition takes a different approach to the Revelation.[10] In mystical sources, the Revelation at Sinai is seen as a multifaceted truth which was experienced, grasped and internalized differently by each person precisely because of their individuality. Because each of their souls was unique, each

---

9. In his *Guide for the Perplexed* (2:35), Maimonides discusses the superiority of Moshe's prophetic ability, which became manifest at the Revelation.
10. Recanati, *Shemot* 20:1.

member of the assembled nation perceived the Revelation in their own unique way, and the truth of the Revelation spoke to them and touched their souls in a unique way.

According to this mystical approach, the multifaceted nature of the Revelation—of truth itself—explains how and why the ongoing halachic and exegetical processes that expound upon the Torah contain so many different opinions: They reflect diverse perceptions of the Word of God. All are legitimate, and all are part of a whole, just as each individual that stood at Sinai was part of one unified nation.

Our challenge is to perceive opinions that differ from our own as containing a glimpse of Divinity, a different aspect of truth that had eluded our grasp. We must find within ourselves the love and strength to value and cherish those divergent opinions, as well as the individuals who express them. This is the lesson of the strange wording of the verses leading up to the Revelation: Unity, not uniformity, made the Revelation at Sinai possible. At that moment in our history, we were able to unite in our diversity. Against that backdrop, the Revelation, which was uniquely perceived by each member of the community, became a possibility. In appreciating and respecting one another's individuality, the Revelation allowed the new nation to achieve unity. Each individual understood that the Revelation experienced by every other person was unique, different than his or her own experience—and equally true, equally valuable.

Unfortunately, human nature seems prone to attack what is different, whether it be a difference in the color of skin, the type of clothing, or the ideas espoused by others. If we are to learn to value others, we must constantly be aware that their "differentness" may be revealing to us a facet of truth that our own souls somehow missed. We must strive to maintain the sense of family that we brought with us to Egypt: A healthy family learns to accept each member as an individual. Not all the children need have the same interests for a family to be loving and respectful. When we accept different ideas and attitudes, we find that the things which unite us are stronger than any of the things that challenge our unity. Just as the heartbeat sustains all the parts of the body, each with its unique role and function, so, too, the heart of the Jewish People must beat with unity—but not necessarily uniformity.

Parashat Mishpatim
Even from the Altar

In the chapters that immediately precede this week's Torah portion, the Ten Commandments rang out from Mount Sinai in a symphony of sound and vision, thunder and lightning—and the world was forever changed. Although the *parashah* we read this week lacks the pyrotechnic accompaniment, its message is a clear continuation of those ten teachings.

The topics covered in *Parashat Mishpatim* seem familiar: Slavery, parents, murder, Shabbat observance, and more, giving us the sense that this is not a new communication, as much as a qualification and extension, or even a clarification of the consequences of violating the commandments taught at Sinai. While the Ten Commandments created value judgments, in *Parashat Mishpatim* these same principles are viewed through a judicial lens: Legal implications are clarified, sanctions and punishments are set out, and the "price" of sin is established.

There is, however, another common strand between *Yitro* and *Mishpatim*; it is a subtle point expressed in a Talmudic perspective of the Revelation at Sinai (*Kiddushin* 31a): The first four commandments may be seen as a cluster of laws that establish fidelity to God and prohibit the worship of any other deity. In and of themselves, these laws would not have seemed

A Taste of Eden

strange to any of the societies or religions of the ancient world. Ancient cultures were well acquainted with jealous gods, and the turf wars and struggles for supremacy among them. The commandments calling for exclusivity may have seemed nothing more than self-serving legislation, and thus unexceptional.

And then, something extraordinary happens: The Fifth Commandment upends all prior concepts of religion. In what seems to be an abrupt change of focus, our mysterious, incorporeal God commands us to honor our parents. With this statement, the nations of the world realized that this religion differed from anything they had previously encountered. This was something new. This commandment was revolutionary, not only because it mandated a certain degree of power-sharing, but because it introduced an entirely new concept into the religious framework: Filial respect is the point of origin for all interpersonal relationships. By including this among the commandments, God brings human society, and the relationships that constitute society, into the religious sphere— in a radical departure from all other belief systems.

The Ten Commandments subtly and uniquely fuse laws regarding our relationship with God together with laws that deal with social justice, thereby creating an entirely new world view. The religious experience and the decency upon which we are commanded to build our interpersonal relationships are no longer to be seen as two diverse realms; rather, they are two aspects of one whole. The Fifth Commandment indicates that these two spheres are intertwined, inseparable. This is the radical, revolutionary message of the Revelation at Sinai.

Reading the verses of *Parashat Mishpatim* with this new understanding of the Ten Commandments reveals new and

Parashat Mishpatim

important insights. For example, the treatment of murder at the outset of the *parashah*: The Sixth Commandment proscribes murder; this is a value statement transmitted at Mount Sinai. In *Parashat Mishpatim*, the specific contours of what constitutes murder are addressed. Categories are created—manslaughter, premeditated murder, criminal negligence, crimes of passion and more; various cases and scenarios are clarified, and punishments are established. In a very clear and unequivocal manner, murder is distinguished from manslaughter, and the punishments for each are set: A person who unintentionally causes the death of his fellow man is removed from society, and sent to a place of refuge. On the other hand, a person guilty of premeditated murder must pay with his or her own life; there is no refuge for a murderer. "If a person plots against his neighbor to kill him intentionally, then you must even take him from My altar to put him to death" (21:13-14).

The reference to the Sanctuary, the holiest place on earth, the epicenter of religious practice, in a verse discussing the basest human behavior, speaks precisely to our newfound insight: A person cannot hide behind their religious appearance or displays of piety if they have committed a crime. Ritual does not eclipse morality; these are two sides of the same proverbial coin, and they cannot exist independently.

This same idea was hinted at in the verses following the Ten Commandments: "When you eventually build a stone altar for Me, do not build it out of cut stone. Your sword will have been lifted against it; you will have profaned it" (20:22). Metal is a symbol of war and mayhem; therefore, it cannot be used to prepare an altar for the service of God. The Sanctuary must be a place not only of worship, not only of ritual purity, but also of peace and social justice. Murderers will find no sanctuary or protection there, nor will it be built with the use of the sword. Similarly, the Ten Commandments do more than address social justice alongside cultic ritual. They meld these two heretofore unrelated aspects of the human experience, teaching us that it is the combination of the two that creates a holy society.

With this understanding of the Revelation, the verses in *Parashat Mishpatim* take on a deeper meaning: The taking of a life is not merely an offense against an individual or even against society as a whole. It is also an offense against God Himself. Man is created in the image of God, formed by God out of the earth He collected from the very spot upon which the Altar would stand (Rashi, *Bereishit* 2:7). In other words, we are not "stardust"; we are the Altar and Holy Temple. The sanctity of human life and the sanctity of the Altar are one and the same. The ritual and the social aspects of holiness spring from the very same source; they are inseparable. Therefore, a person who takes a life will not find refuge in the Sanctuary.

Judaism's revolutionary vision of holiness, then, is that ritual and social holiness are two sides of one coin, two parts of the same Tablets. The Ten Commandments were the first harbingers of this vision, and the verses of *Parashat Mishpatim* translate that vision into law.

Parashat Terumah
The View from Above

As *Parashat Terumah* begins, we are somewhat taken aback: Out of nowhere, instructions for a major construction project are handed down. In place of the very practical torts discussed in the previous *parashah*—laws necessary for the proper functioning of society—now laws regarding building an edifice are transmitted, and in great detail. The focus has clearly shifted from creating an elevated society to the service of God. Admittedly these concepts need not be mutually exclusive, but the dramatic shift cannot be ignored.

There was, however, an important segue which might easily have been missed: *Mishpatim* did not conclude with the aforementioned torts; rather, the final scene shows Moshe climbing the cloud-enveloped mountain, preparing for his rendezvous with God. The instructions to build the Mishkan follow. Our conclusion is that the laws transmitted in *Parashat Terumah* should be read as a continuation of the narrative at the end of *Parashat Mishpatim:* These instructions were given to Moshe when he arrived at the top of the mountain, at his perch in the clouds, a place closer to heaven than to earth.

Building a Mishkan, or a Temple, is a means of linking heaven and earth. How appropriate, then, that the instructions to build the first Mishkan were only given when Moshe scaled the mountain and could see things from above.

In a sense, this is like the ladder of Yaakov's vision, with its feet on the ground and its head in the sky—creating the image of the connection between heaven and earth. When Yaakov awakes from his dream and vows to build a house of God, his vow seems a logical and fitting conclusion :

> Yaakov awoke from his sleep. He said, "God is truly in this place, but I did not know it." He was frightened. "How awe-inspiring this place is!" he exclaimed. "It must be God's temple. It is the gate to heaven!" (*Bereishit* 28:16-17)

Yaakov sees a ladder; he sees the angels ascending and descending. Apparently, he, like Moshe, sees the view from above; in fact, he and Moshe see exactly the same thing from that heavenly vantage point: a temple.

Our Sages teach us that Yaakov saw this vision as he lay in the vicinity of Jerusalem, whereas Moshe saw this vision when he climbed Mount Sinai—the place where the people experienced unparalleled unity. This unity is what made the Revelation of Sinai possible: Like the Sinai experience itself, a Torah scroll becomes invalid ("unkosher") if even one letter is missing. The Torah represents the totality of the Jewish people. When we lack unity, we deny something fundamental about the Torah itself —even to the point that we ourselves "invalidate" or "destroy" it.

Similarly, the Temple represents the unity of the people. When the people are fractured, the very walls of the Temple

Parashat Terumah

crack and crumble. One of the fundamental teachings regarding the destruction of the Temple is that it was brought about by disunity, "unwarranted hatred" between us.

The archetype of disunity was the hatred of Yosef by his brothers. Perhaps this was why their father Yaakov, despite his vow, was unable to actualize his vision and construct the physical walls of this edifice. The hatred within his household would have destroyed this temple; in fact, it prevented its construction altogether.

At Sinai, the people stood as one and accepted the Torah, the blueprint for creating an elevated and enlightened society. At that shining moment in history, they were inspired, and called out, "*na'aseh ve-nishma*," "We will do and we will listen!" (*Shemot* 24:7) This newfound unity created a new opportunity to build the Temple. Only now had Yaakov's children achieved the unity that would enable them to fulfill Yaakov's vow; God said: "They shall make Me a sanctuary, and I will dwell among them" (*Shemot* 25:8).

God will only dwell among us if we are united. At Sinai, at long last, unity was achieved. Together with adherence to the laws of Torah, the Sanctuary—and later, the Temple—would be a way to sustain that unity.

Standing above the clouds, half way to heaven, everything was perfectly clear: We have the ability to connect heaven and earth, the sacred and the mundane. The first step toward this endeavor is not the building of a Temple; rather, it is the unity of the people who will utilize it to worship God. Only as a united nation are we able to share Yaakov's vision of the ladder—the link between heaven and earth.

Parashat Tetzaveh
Holy Clothing

The chapters immediately preceding this *parashah* contained very precise instructions for building the Mishkan (Sanctuary). Now, our attention is turned to those who will serve as its custodians: the *kohanim*. *Parashat Tetzaveh* records, in minute detail, God's instructions for the creation of the special clothing to be worn by the *kohanim*, and in particular the *kohen gadol* (High Priest). Apparently, entry into the holy domain, and especially into the Holy of Holies, the innermost sanctum of the Mishkan, required preparation; the garments described in this *parashah* served as an outward manifestation of this internal, spiritual preparation.

Talmudic tradition offers an additional insight into the symbolic nature of these garments, matching each one with the particular sin for which it is meant to bring about forgiveness.[11] And yet, the connection between clothing and sin is not immediately clear. While we know that clothing can be seductive, and may lead to certain types of sin, it can also be used to obscure, to restrict, or even to oppress. This focus on clothing and its association with sin, however, is not new to

---

11. See Talmud *Zevachim* 88b; *Archin* 16a; *Kereitot* 27b.

Parashat Tetzaveh

this section of the Torah; in fact, it goes as far back as the very beginning of time.

In the Garden of Eden, Adam and Eve were without clothing, without shame—and without sin. Only in a post-sin reality—a reality with which we are well acquainted—is clothing needed. It is no accident that the etymology of a number of Hebrew words that describe articles of clothing connects them to sin: The word *beged* (garment) comes from the root *bagad* (betrayal). Similarly, *me'il* (coat) is connected to *me'ilah* (misappropriation). According to the Talmud, the word for clothing, *levush*, is comprised of two words, *lo bosh*, "shall not be embarrassed."[12] The sin in Eden, then, as it is reflected in these words, was both a betrayal and a misappropriation. When this first sin was committed, the need for clothing arose: Mankind, once innocent and honest, now required, both literally and figuratively, a "cover-up."

As we know, exile from the Garden of Eden did not bring an end to sin. In the very next generation, the symbolic connection between sin and clothing deepened: Cain, a farmer, murdered his brother Abel, a shepherd, and according to rabbinic tradition, this heinous crime lies at the heart of the prohibition of *shaatnez*; the Torah prohibits the mixing of wool, a product of the flocks, with linen, an agricultural product. We are commanded to ensure that in our clothing, the divergent realms of Cain and Abel are not combined.[13] Our clothing not only reflects the sin, but is intended to serve as a constant reminder and symbolic wake-up call.

12. Talmud *Shabbat* 77b. For more on this topic see my *Echoes of Eden* (Jerusalem: Gefen Publishing and OU Press, 2011), especially *Parashat Vayeshev*, "Clothes Make the Man," p. 245.
13. *Midrash Tanchuma, Bereishit*, section 9.

A Taste of Eden

The Mishkan, and later the Beit HaMikdash (Temple), were intended to be places of healing and rapprochement. There, man could approach God and seek forgiveness. No wonder, then, that a representation of mankind before sin stood in the holiest place within the Sanctuary: The *keruvim*, two angelic cherubs, simulacra of Adam and Eve in their original state of innocence,[14] hovered over the Holy Ark. These innocent, naked figurines represented man before he corrupted himself and his world, before shame and guilt created a need for clothing. However, in order to enter this area, the *Kohen Gadol* had to be dressed in "holy clothing," not merely to serve as a fig leaf to cover his nakedness, but as a profound acknowledgment of the human condition in a world corrupted by sin.

On the other hand, this same clothing contained within it a statement of hope: Unlike all other clothing, the garments of the *kohen* were made of a combination of linen and wool. Symbolically, the *kohen* was not limited by the repercussions of Cain's sin; the Torah specifies that this clothing is to be made of *shaatnez*. Only one day a year, on Yom Kippur, when the *Kohen Gadol* entered the Holy of Holies and the *keruvim* were in full view, were these clothes of *shaatnez* set aside. On this special day, all ornaments, all distractions, all symbols of sin were stripped away. On Yom Kippur, the *Kohen Gadol* wore clothes of pure white, in an attempt to reach the level of purity that he would see when he beheld the naked *keruvim* within the inner sanctum. Neither clothing of gold, representing the sin of the golden calf, nor *shaatnez*, representing the murder of Abel, could cross that

---

14. See my *Explorations* (Southfield, MI: Targum Press, 2001), p. 169 for a broader discussion of this topic.

Parashat Tetzaveh

threshold. For in that unique place, reconciliation between Cain and Abel suddenly became possible, just as reconciliation with God suddenly came with man's reach.

Parashat Ki Tisa (Purim)
Knowing Tomorrow

At the foot of Mount Sinai—the very same spot where the most awesome events had unfolded a mere forty days earlier—the people were anxious. Moshe, their leader, had not come down, and fear for his survival spread throughout the camp.

What happens next seems inconceivable on so many levels: How could a nation that had witnessed the miraculous plagues in Egypt and the splitting of the sea, a nation whose daily sustenance, the manna, descended for them each morning from heaven, a nation that had seen the heavens open up, a nation that had witnessed God with their own senses—nonetheless question and defy God?

> The people saw that Moshe was taking a long time to come down from the mountain. They gathered around Aharon and said to him, "Make for us a god to lead us, for Moshe, the man who brought us out of Egypt we do not know what happened to him." (*Shemot* 32:1)

This verse is comprised of two distinct elements, two hints that may provide us with insights into this terrible sin. Moshe's disappearance is clearly the trigger for this rapid devolution, but the words with which the people express themselves are very specific: In what appears to be a strange cause-and-effect strategy on their part, they turn to Aharon and ask him to "make a god" because they "do not know" what happened to Moshe. Of these two elements, the solution they suggest for their predicament, the making of a god, is surely more disturbing, because it is a direct violation of the Second Commandment which they had recently received. However, there is a common thread between these two elements that harks back to a time and place much earlier than Sinai. Both of these elements—the question of knowledge about Moshe's fate, and the desire to make a god to solve the problem, were, in fact, elements of the very first sin at the dawn of history:

> God knows that on the day you eat from it, your eyes will be opened, and you will be like god, knowing good and evil. (*Bereishit* 3:5)

From time immemorial, mankind has suffered from delusions of grandeur, and has been unable or unwilling to accept the vast chasm that separates man and God. The very first verses of the Torah sketch the outlines of human intellectual hubris: Mankind has always assumed that all types of knowledge are accessible, that we have the inalienable right to know and understand everything, without exception. This attitude is just as obvious in the Garden of Eden as it is at the foot of Mount Sinai.

And so, as Aharon faces this new-fangled expression of an age-old spiritual malady, his first line of defense is a delaying tactic. He instructs the dissolute mob to bring the jewelry belonging to their spouses and children. One can only assume that this very specific task, and not a more general order to bring gold and whatever precious metals they had at hand, was devised in the hope that the wives and children would form the first line of defense: If not for religious reasons, then at least out of far more pragmatic concern for their valuables, they might dissuade the mob. The text gives no clear indication whether the wives acquiesced[15] or if, along with the other outrages committed that day, theft of personal property was an additional charge on the rap sheet.

Aharon sees how the golden calf is formed and he declares that a holiday for God will be observed on the following day. A very careful reading of Aharon's response indicates that it is far more complex than we might have assumed. First, Aharon declares the holiday in the name of the Eternal God, making pointed and specific use of the ineffable name that describes God as transcendent and unknowable. We can only assume that Aharon's intention was to point out the absurdity of worshipping the newly-forged golden calf. The second element of Aharon's response is, once again, a stalling tactic—pushing off the celebration for the following day, in order to cool down their hotheaded, visceral enthusiasm and allow clearer thinking to prevail.

This stalling tactic had been used not long before, when the tribe of Amalek descended upon them in a murderous campaign against God and His people. Moshe appointed Yehoshua to fight Amalek, but, oddly enough, instructed him

---

15. "All the people took off their earrings and brought them to Aharon" (*Shemot* 32:3).

Parashat Ki Tisa (Purim)

to respond to the Amalekite assault only on the following day.[16] Quite purposefully, the element of delayed gratification was used as a weapon against Amalek, the descendants of Esav. Like their forefather, their hallmark was immediate gratification. Esav lived in the here-and-now, and bartered the future for a bowl of beans, scorning a birthright that included hundreds of years of slavery in return for the rights to the Land of Israel. Similarly, Amalek pounced upon the descendants of Yaakov as they were poised to enter the Land of Israel, after having paid their dues in Egypt—but the mighty tribe of Amalek was unable to vanquish a nation of emancipated slaves who were willing to take the long road. Moshe's instructions to Yehoshua taught us that the way to combat Esav's immediate-gratification mentality is to focus on the future, to place our faith in the Eternal God.

Now, Aharon uses the same strategy against the murderous,[17] idolatrous mob—the only difference being that this time, the mob is his own people; this time, we ourselves are our own worst enemy. We had become like Amalek, seeking immediate answers and solutions, and we received the same treatment.

The same is true of the events of Purim, generations after the golden calf debacle: Haman, a descendant of Amalek, nearly succeeded in destroying the Jewish People in order to fulfill his insatiable desire for immediate gratification. The Jews

---

16. We usually understand that the war began immediately, although Moshe, Aharon, and Hur did not respond in prayer until the next day. However, rabbinic sources teach that this verse is among those that remain "unresolved" as to whether the word "tomorrow" is part of the orders to Yehoshua ("Go fight Amalek tomorrow") or part of the narrative regarding Moshe, Hur, and Aharon ("Go and fight Amalek; tomorrow, etc."). See *Mekhilta de-Rabbi Yishmael, Amalek*, section 1.

17. Tradition records that the mob murdered Hur when he attempted to stop them. See Rashi, *Shemot* 32:5.

had become vulnerable precisely because they had adopted the Amalekite mindset, becoming willing participants in the hedonistic and idolatrous lifestyle of Shushan. Queen Esther understood that the remedy for our spiritual vulnerability hinged upon our ability to battle Esav and Amalek through our faith in the Eternal, in the spiritual life that goes beyond the here-and-now orientation of our enemies. She insured that the battle against Esav-Amalek-Haman would take place not only on the day Haman had decreed for the battle, but on the following day as well.

We celebrate this victory *ad de-lo yada*—until we understand that we cannot know everything. There are things that remain beyond the grasp of human intellect; these are the things that give rise to our faith in *Netzach Yisrael,* the Eternal God of Israel.

Happy Purim!

Parshiyot Vayakhel–Pekudei
An Accounting

As the Book of *Shemot* draws to a conclusion, so, too, does the building of the Mishkan. The detailed instructions for the Mishkan and the account of its actual construction dominate the last third of the Book of *Shemot*, and both the book and the building project end in these twinned *parshiyot*.

As the supreme leader, Moshe bears responsibility for the project as a whole, even though the verses recount that the actual construction of the structure and the creation of the various utensils that it housed were delegated to a number of highly skilled and divinely-inspired artisans.

As the Mishkan nears completion, Moshe gives a complete accounting of all the raw materials that had been collected and a full record of how these materials were used. These particular verses might seem somewhat redundant, as they are preceded by a similar catalogue of the raw materials as they were collected. Rabbinic tradition offers an unexpected, even surprising rationale for the inclusion of this seemingly-unnecessary inventory: Remarkably, the midrash[18] recounts the idle chatter which cynically cast Moshe in the most negative light, accusing him of personally benefiting from the project, and living off

---

18. *Midrash Tanchuma, Parashat Pekudei* (Buber edition, section 4).

the communal till. These accusations are particularly ironic, for they accuse Moshe of eating the choicest cuts of meats, ostensibly procured unethically. The irony, of course, lies in the fact that when Moshe ascended Mount Sinai, first to receive the Torah and then to beg for forgiveness on behalf of the nation that had worshipped the golden calf, he did not eat or drink for forty days and forty nights. Moshe was so far beyond the sort of hedonistic excess of which the gossip accused him, it seems almost comical—yet the sheer absurdity of the insinuations did not keep tongues from wagging.

The Talmud[19] points out another example of this same sort of gossip: Moshe, the holiest man who ever lived, was accused of conducting himself immorally with numerous women in the Israelite camp. Apparently, the origin of the accusation was the fidelity which the women had for Moshe—and, in turn for God. The major sins committed in the desert were perpetrated by the men; tradition teaches us that the women did not take part. They remained pure. The men interpreted this strange fidelity in the most sordid and sexually charged manner; this, it seems, was the only way they could understand the "bizarre" hold Moshe had on those who stayed committed to God.

Once again, the irony is inescapable: Moshe remained in a state of perpetual preparedness to receive the Word of God. Just as the Israelites were instructed to abstain from spousal intimacy in preparation for the Revelation at Sinai, so, too, Moshe maintained an elevated state of ritual purity because his communication with God was constant, imminent, unforeseen.[20] Moshe remained at the level of purity and spiritual

19. Talmud Bavli, *Sanhedrin* 110a.
20. See Rashi, *Bemidbar* 12:1.

preparedness that the nation as a whole maintained for three days at the foot of Mount Sinai, because he could not know when his next prophetic experience would take place.[21]

How cynical, then, was the gossip of his day: The man who separated from his wife, who dedicated his life to the spiritual enlightenment of his nation, who remained always poised to receive the Divine Word, was accused of illicit relationships with other men's wives. Similarly, the man who refrained from all food and drink was accused of gluttony at the public's expense.

Moshe, for his part, gives a public accounting of all monies and materials collected and spent, setting a high standard indeed for all future leaders and for the use and treatment of public funds. Despite his impeccable behavior, cynics and sinners would always seek out flaws in his personal behavior, and fabricate what they could not find. Only the most jaundiced eyes could create shadows of excess and licentiousness in their attempts to eclipse Moshe's greatness, casting aspersions in the very areas of his extraordinary restraint.

God, however, expresses complete trust in Moshe:

This is not true of My servant Moshe, who is the most faithful of all in My house. (*Bemidbar* 12:7)

Specifically, here, where he is under attack, we understand just how wise Moshe was: Despite the unparalleled testament of confidence and trust in him by God Himself, Moshe knew that people were not as generous. God Himself attested to Moshe's trustworthiness, but Moshe was wise enough not to let that

---

21. One midrash traces Moshe's behavior to the revelation at the burning bush. See *Sifri Zuta, Bemidbar* chapter 12.

A Taste of Eden

testimonial stand alone. He gave a complete, public accounting, fulfilling the commandment that binds each of us, particularly our leaders, to the highest ethical standards:

To be clean before God and Israel. (*Bemidbar* 32:22)

Parashat Vayikra
Regrets

Regrets, I've had a few
But then again, too few to mention
I did what I had to do and saw it through without
  exemption
I planned each charted course, each careful step along the
  byway
And more, much more than this, I did it my way.
— Written by Paul Anka for Frank Sinatra

Modern man, increasingly the product of moral relativism, looks at life with few regrets. "After all," the logic goes, "I am who I am because of the path I have taken. Had I taken a different path, I would not be me, nor would I be true to myself." This semi-deterministic attitude, seasoned with a sizable dose of narcissism, leaves us fully accepting the choices we have made and the people we have become.

In fact, it may be said that only the "losers" in modern society regret their mistakes. Only they are made to feel guilty of having made colossal errors, whereas the missteps of the rich and famous are more often than not parlayed into the all-too-familiar circus of rehab, followed by a tell-all memoir, followed

A Taste of Eden

by talk-show appearances and assorted opportunities for public catharsis. The message is that when bad choices, poor judgment, self-indulgence and abusive behavior go too far, they may require reining-in or containment, but no regret is necessary.

The new world presented in this week's *parashah* stands in contrast to this regret-free mindset. The Mishkan, and the sacrificial offerings that would be brought there, become a part of the Israelites' reality in *Parashat Vayikra*. In a sense, we may say that mistakes—errors in judgment, oversights, sins large and small—lie at the very core of this holy edifice; the Mishkan is created in order to redress human failure. On the other hand, the world in which the Mishkan exists is a world in which change is possible, a world that breaks through the complacency of accepting oneself "as is," a world in which we can strive to correct our failings.

The Mishkan does not provide healing from deliberate sin; premeditated offenses are not expunged by offerings. The "sin offerings," for the most part, atone for transgressions committed accidentally, when the major offense was thoughtlessness of one kind or another. The experience of bringing an offering is intended to lead to heightened awareness and increased responsibility, on an intellectual level, for ones' actions. The entire system of *mitzvot* is intended to create human beings that function on a higher level of cognitive awareness and spiritual alertness. We are enjoined to march through life not as automatons or as creatures of instinct or habit; rather, we are expected to be constantly thinking of the consequences of our actions. Intellectual sloth leads to a dulled sense of personal responsibility; this, in turn, will lead to the necessity for atonement, through sin offerings in the Mishkan.

Parashat Vayikra

The *korban olah* (elevation offering), the very first offering listed in this *parashah*, is particularly instructive. This offering is generally brought as recompense, not for a violation of one of the negative commandments, but as a means of reconnecting with God after failing to fulfill a positive commandment. The *olah* is an offering for a mitzvah that was not performed. It is an expression of regret for the good that was not achieved.

Both the thought process and the ethic taught by the *korbanot* can be transformative—even for those of us who only read about them in the Torah but are unable to experience them firsthand. As opposed to our society, where we are taught that all of our shortcomings can be attributed to every possible external factor, the world of *korbanot* places the blame squarely on the shoulders of the person who made the mistake, particularly when that mistake was accidental. More responsibility, not less, is called for; heightened alertness, a higher level of consciousness, more finely-attuned thoughtfulness, are the tools that enable us to avoid future transgressions—but that is not all.

The Judaic view of a perfected society is not a world in which we simply err less; avoiding sin is only part of the equation. In addition, we are commanded to constantly question whether we are doing enough good. Have we missed opportunities to do *mitzvot*? Have we been negligent or lazy, thus allowing a deficiency to exist in the world—a deficiency of good that we could have or should have filled? A very basic tenet of our faith encapsulates this dual mandate: "Distance yourself from evil and do good, pray for peace and pursue it" (Psalm 34:15).

The point of origin of the Book of *Vayikra* is the *korban olah*, a sacrifice that expresses regret for a missed opportunity to do good, to bring goodness into our lives and the lives of those around us. In a world in which we quickly forgive our own foibles, the Torah challenges us to look inside ourselves with humility and honesty, and to ask ourselves if we have done enough good. If the answer is "no," we are instructed to bring an *olah*—an offering from which man derives no physical benefit. The *korban olah* is a burnt offering, dedicated entirely to God— just as we should be. When we internalize the lesson of this offering, we have taken the first steps on the path to a perfected world—a world with less error, but, no less importantly, a world with much more good.

Parashat Tzav
Matzah and Chametz

The concepts of leavened and unleavened bread are familiar to us from the holiday of Passover, but we tend to focus on the physical or technical aspects that differentiate them from one another. However, Jewish tradition goes far beyond the physics of the dough itself, and seeks out the deeper symbolism of *chametz* and matzah.

Talmudic teachings regarding Passover associate leavened bread with the evil inclination:[22] The difference between leavened bread, *chametz*, and matzah, the unleavened "bread of poverty," is that bread is puffed up, indicating haughtiness or pride. And yet, this teaching leads to some unavoidable questions: If bread is associated with negative attributes, why should it ever be allowed? Why not require that we eat only unleavened bread all year round? Alternatively, we may ask, why is Passover specifically the time to prohibit leavened bread? Furthermore, while we can easily understand the obligation to eat matzah to commemorate our hasty departure from Egypt, we should have no difficulty imagining that this symbolic food might co-exist with leavened bread. In other words, why prohibit bread simply because we are obligated to eat matzah?

22. Talmud Bavli *Berachot* 17a, and commentary of Rashi ad loc.

A Taste of Eden

In order to address these questions, we would do well to broaden our scope to include another festival that is intrinsically linked to Passover: Shavuot, the Festival of Weeks. While the Exodus from Egypt serves as the catalyst for the prohibition of bread, we are commanded to count seven weeks, and on the fiftieth day to celebrate Shavuot, thus creating an unbreakable chronological link between the two holidays. While we may say that the primary link between Passover and Shavuot lies in their agricultural aspects, the theological, historical and symbolic aspects of these festivals are no less intertwined: Specifically, on Shavuot, as opposed to every other day of the year, bread is included in the service and celebratory sacrifice in the Beit HaMikdash. Seen from this perspective, the link between Passover and Shavuot creates a continuum, shedding light on the questions we have raised regarding *chametz* and matzah, as it leads us from the prohibition of bread to the occasion on which leavened bread is brought into the Temple service.

In fact, the Torah laws that govern the sacrifices brought throughout the year in the Beit HaMikdash bring our questions into even sharper focus: As a rule, other than the *shtei ha-lechem*, the two loaves that are an integral part of the service on Shavuot, bread was not allowed in the Temple or Temple service at all. This week's *parashah* contains a clear statement of this prohibition:

> Aharon and his descendants shall then eat the rest [of the offering]. It must be eaten as unleavened bread in a holy place. They must therefore eat it in the enclosure of the Tent of Meeting. It shall not be baked as leavened bread. I have given this to them as their portion in My

fire offerings, and it is holy of holies, like the sin offering and the guilt offering.... (*Vayikra* 6:9-10)

Other than the two loaves offered on Shavuot, there is only one other exception to the ban on leavened bread in the Temple, and it, too, is found in this week's *parashah*:

> And this is the law of the peace offering that is sacrificed to God: If it is offered as a thanksgiving offering, then it must be presented along with unleavened loaves mixed with oil, flat *matzahs* saturated with oil, and loaves made of a boiled mixture of flour and oil. The sacrifice shall also be presented along with loaves of leavened bread; all these shall be brought with one's thanksgiving peace offering. (*Vayikra* 7:11-13)

This unique combination of breads is offered in thanksgiving: When an individual feels that his or her life has been spared through Divine intervention, when a personal catastrophe is averted and a person experiences personal salvation, they may bring this offering of gratitude to celebrate the peace they have been granted. It is specifically this thanksgiving "peace offering" that includes both leavened and unleavened bread.

We have learned two apparently independent laws, one regarding the unique service on Shavuot and one regarding the thanksgiving sacrifice; when we overlay these two laws, a fascinating observation emerges: The Passover experience, encompassing the paschal sacrifice, the matzah, even the Seder itself, may be akin to a "thanksgiving" offering. If this is the case, we cannot help but notice that something is missing, and

A Taste of Eden

the thanksgiving is not complete: The leavened bread that is an integral part of the thanksgiving offering is not included in the celebration of Passover. Quite the opposite: Leavened bread is strictly prohibited throughout the entire festival, leading us to the conclusion that despite our feelings of thanksgiving and joy, we are really not quite completely free. The national and personal freedom that Passover celebrates is somehow lacking, hence the inclusion of leavened bread is inappropriate.

What is missing from the Passover story? Why is our celebration, and our offering, less than perfect? When the Jews left Egypt, they were politically free, yet they were spiritually limited. They were wrested from the depths of depraved Egyptian society, extricated from the world of idolatry and superstition, yet no other belief system had taken the place of the idolatry they left behind.

The prohibition of bread on Passover reminds us that leaving Egypt was not enough. Physical, political freedom is simply a means to an end; we were not truly free until we were given our mandate, until we accepted our mission, until we appreciated the *raison d'être* for our liberation from Egypt. Only when we stood at Sinai and accepted the Torah was our liberation complete. As we celebrate Passover, we mark a time when we were still a humble nation of emancipated slaves who had not yet achieved true freedom. Only after accepting the Torah, after accepting our new marching orders, after accepting the loftiest mission given to humankind, was there place for pride.

Only on Shavuot can we celebrate and give thanks for our complete freedom and take pride in our partnership with God, a partnership designed to elevate and transform the world. On

Parashat Tzav

Shavuot, we complete our thanksgiving, adding the two loaves of leavened bread that were missing on Passover. This sort of celebration, in which we complete our offering of thanksgiving, is reserved for those who enjoy true freedom. Celebrating anything less is a shallow celebration of mediocrity.

Passover
Becoming a Nation

Passover commemorates the liberation of the Israelites from Egypt. The Exodus, however, was not exclusively a transformation in the realm of workers' rights and workplace conditions. Something else monumental happened as a result of their freedom: A new nation came into being. The Jewish People was born.

The arrival the sons of Yaakov in Egypt came about because of dysfunctionality in the family: Ten of his brothers sold Yosef, who became a slave. Little did the brothers know that Yosef's personal journey would pave the way for their own trip to Egypt, where their own families would, in turn, be enslaved.

Oppression has a way of stripping away one's individual identity; apparently this is equally true of national identity. And yet, against all odds, this family/tribe increased in numbers, even though they lacked any of the real markers of peoplehood. If the logic of history were the only factor in play, we would never have heard of this family again—one of any number of extended families that came down to Egypt for sustenance in a time of famine. Yet rather than being subsumed into Egypt, this tribe morphed into something else—something not clearly

Passover

defined. And then, one magical and exalted night, the Children of Israel became a nation.

The vicissitudes of Jewish history, the highs and lows of our national story, have created different types of Passover experiences. At times, we celebrated our independence; other times, we could do no more than reminisce or yearn for our freedom. When Jews were able to observe Passover in our national homeland, the celebration was more like a spiritual-social-political "independence day," replete with religious symbolism and imbued and defined by ritual. On the other hand, for thousands of years and at all corners of the earth, Passover has also been celebrated in the diaspora, where it serves as a celebration of the past and an expression of hope for the future. Passover in the Warsaw ghetto was not the same as Passover in Jerusalem, the capital of the Jewish nation-state.

Yet one element seems to unite these divergent Passover celebrations: Passover is always about family, tribe, and nation—in that order. Family is the core of any nascent tribe; families are the building blocks of a nation, yet one of the risks of nationhood is the loss of the individual in macro, "big picture" considerations. The celebration of Passover combats this danger by building the religious experience from the ground up, as it were: Tribal identification, starting with the nuclear family and spreading to include the extended family, lies at the core of Passover observance.

Strangely enough, the very first stage of the Passover story, the point of origin of our bondage, is left unspoken on this night. The tale of the sons of Yaakov is one of familial dysfunction— and that is what the experience of Passover is designed to correct. The message, subtly conveyed through the structure

117

A Taste of Eden

of Seder night, is simply this: Our nation is only as strong as its component parts, and the starting point is family. Only as a family are we able to internalize and integrate the concepts of slavery and liberation.

Accepting upon ourselves the moral responsibility created by our collective memory of oppression and otherness informs the most basic levels of our national personality. The responsibility we take upon ourselves makes us who we are: Not merely a collective that is based on shared experiences, no matter how formative, but a collective that shares a dream of salvation—for each and every one of us, one family at a time.

This shared vision of the past and the future (along with savory food) has made the Passover Seder the longest-running educational program in the history of the world. The Seder experience unites Jews vertically and horizontally, across the divisional generation gap and across tribal lines, creating the glorious mosaic that is one large family, one united tribe, one inspired nation.

Parashat Shmini
You Are What You Eat

One of the distinguishing practices of Jewish observance is the distinct set of dietary considerations that constitutes the laws of *kashrut*.

In the early chapters of the Torah, the prohibition against eating any part of a live animal is introduced—not as a "Jewish" law, but rather as a universal practice. Later, in the chapters that detail the formation of the Jewish People, the law requiring separation between milk and meat—specifically, the commandment not to "cook a kid in its mother's milk"—is repeated several times. Subsequently, prohibitions against the consumption of blood and certain fats were added.

In the book of *Vayikra*, in *Parashat Shmini*, we are presented with a long and detailed list of prohibited and permitted animals, fowl and fish. The list is not accompanied by any explanatory verses; all of the laws of *kashrut* are given without rhyme or reason. These particular laws are generally characterized by the term *chok* or "statute," a biblical term used to denote a decree, something beyond the constructs of human logic—the type of law that man never would have intuited or created in the context of the "social contract."

119

A Taste of Eden

The propriety or even the permissibility of searching for reasons for such laws is debated among the commentaries; we are, by definition, incapable of understanding God's motives in creating these laws. On the other hand, many of our greatest sages encouraged all those who observe these laws to enhance their understanding of them from the human perspective: Rather than asking *why* God decreed that our diet should be governed by these specific rules, rather than asking *how* these laws affect us and our world, we are encouraged to approach *chukkim* (Divine decrees) from the perspective of the adherent, and to ask, *what* is the spiritual message for me?[23] Subservience to laws of this type may constitute what Kierkegaard labeled a "leap of faith," but the subjective religious experience of the practitioner lies in the realm of the individual's intellectual, emotional, and spiritual engagement with the mitzvah.

Dietary laws illustrate this distinction: The prohibition against eating a severed limb from a live animal (or, for that matter, severing a limb from a live animal), should require no explanation. Human decency recoils at the very thought of such barbarism, and we require no symbolic interpretation for this universal prohibition. On the other hand, the prohibition against mixing milk and meat is not intrinsically repugnant in this way, and requires us to consider less literal levels of meaning: Milk is symbolic of the flow of life from mother to child. Although the Torah does permit us to eat meat, and, unavoidably, to take the life of an animal for this purpose, there are limitations that must be respected. The prohibition against mixing milk and meat

23. Rabbi Joseph B. Soloveitchik discussed this distinction at length. An adaptation of some of The Rav's lectures on this topic may be found in Chapter 10 of Abraham Besdin's *Man of Faith in the Modern World: Reflections of the Rav*, vol. 2 (1989: Ktav Publishing House, Inc., Hoboken, N.J.).

Parashat Shmini

implies that the flow of life symbolized by milk is incongruous with the consumption of flesh. To combine the two is to create an incongruity that dulls our sensitivity. Thus, although the law is transmitted without a rationale, the symbolism involved in this law speaks to the human condition. We do not ask what God's rationale is, nor do we examine the physical affects and outcomes of observance or non-observance. Instead, we discern a deeper message that impacts our inner spiritual world, and, at the same time, brings us closer to the Creator.

In this same way, we may now approach the laws in *Parashat Shmini*. The list of animals and birds that are deemed non-kosher includes carnivorous species: Although eating meat is allowed, the animals we eat should be herbivores, not carnivores. Additionally, we are permitted to eat only fish that have scales and fins. On a functional level, fins serve an interesting purpose: They allow fish to swim upstream, against the tide.

Perhaps these seemingly arbitrary sets of markers contain a great spiritual message: We are what we eat. We must be careful about the food we ingest, because it becomes a part of us, not only biologically, but also spiritually. Although we are permitted to eat meat, this should not be our defining trait. Furthermore, perhaps fish is an important part of our diet not only because it is a healthy source of protein, but because of the defining characteristic embodied in the signs of *kashrut*: the ability to swim against the tide. This same ability has been a defining trait and an invaluable skill for Jews throughout history. Just as the laws of *kashrut* have, to a great extent, secured our identity as a separate people, our ability to swim against the tide has insured that we are not pulled into oblivion by the shifting tides of time and fashion.

Parashiyot
Tazria–Metzora
Free Bird

The twin Torah portions of *Tazria* and *Metzora* contend with
many physiological phenomena—some commonplace and
natural, others rare and sinister: Everything from childbirth
and common bodily excretions to skin lesions, leprosy
and strange afflictions of garments and homes. Although
these are all physical, if not physiological conditions, the
Torah prescribes a spiritual response: These phenomena
are treated not (or not only) from the obvious physical-
medical perspective, but from what may be called a "Temple
perspective" as well, in which different physical conditions
generate various degrees of distance or separation from the
holy epicenter of the Israelite camp.

Of all the phenomena enumerated in these chapters,
leprosy engenders the most extreme reaction: The leper is
completely separated, not only from society, but from the
Temple as well. Some rabbinic commentaries explain this
quarantine as a safeguard against physical contagion,[24] while

---

24. See comments of Hizkuni, *Vayikra* 13:46.

most commentaries see it as a means of preventing spiritual contagion:[25] Rabbinic tradition connects the leprous condition with inappropriate speech or gossip, hence the need for quarantine/excommunication. In either case, the Torah maps out the road back, a ritual that allows the leper to return, step by step, to society in general, and to the Temple in particular. Closer examination of the details of this ritual offers tremendous insight into the Jewish concept of rehabilitation.

An essential element of the ritual is the offering of two birds (*Vayikra* 14:4). The Talmud explains that the bird and its incessant tweeting is symbolic of the sin of excessive chatter, gossip and idle talk that brought about the leprosy and its resultant punishment of isolation:

R. Samuel b. Nadav, the son-in-law of R. Hanina, asked of R. Hanina (according to others, he asked of R. Yehoshua b. Levi): In what way is the leper different (than other sinners) that the Torah said: "He shall dwell alone; outside of the camp shall his dwelling be?" He (through his gossip) separated a husband from his wife, a man from his neighbor, therefore said the Torah: "He shall dwell alone." R. Yehoshua b. Levi said: In what way is the leper different (from others who require

---

25. Rambam, *Tum'at Tzara'at* 16:10: "*Tzara'at* is a collective term including many afflictions that do not resemble each other. For the whitening of a person's skin is called *tzara'at*, as is the falling out of some of the hair of his head or beard, and the change of the color of clothes or houses. This change that affects clothes and houses which the Torah described with the general term of *tzara'at* is not a natural occurrence. Instead it is a sign and a wonder prevalent among the Jewish people to warn them against *lashon hara* [undesirable speech]...."

penitence) that the Torah said: "[He shall bring] two live clean birds so that he may become pure again'? The Holy One, blessed be He, said: He did the work of a babbler, therefore let him offer a babbler as a sacrifice. (*Arachin* 16b)

The Sages of the Mishnah taught that a specific type of bird was offered in these cases: *dror*.[26] The word *dror* means "freedom"; the birds that the leper brings are "freebirds." In Psalms, the *dror* is identified as the bird that makes its home near the Temple.

How lovely are your dwelling places, O Lord of hosts! My soul longs, indeed it faints for the courts of the Lord; my heart and my flesh cry out for the living God. Even the bird has found a house, the *dror* a nest for herself, where she may lay her young, at Your altars, O Lord of hosts, my King, and my God. Happy are those who dwell in Your house, ever praising you. Selah! (Psalm 84:2-6)

Here, the freebird is a creature that experiences and is aware of its angst, and longs for rehabilitation, a bird that wishes to return home—to the Temple.

This is a far cry from the "freebird" of popular culture, made famous in the rock ballad by Lynyrd Skynyrd. In this view, the free bird is caught in a never-ending cycle of wandering and rootlessness, isolation and seclusion. Above all else, this "freedom" is achieved through the inability or unwillingness to change:

26. Mishnah, *Nega'im* 14:1.

Tazria–Metzora

Lord knows, I can't change
Lord help me, I can't change
Lord I can't change
Won't you fly high free bird, yeah.[27]

The Torah's view of freedom is precisely the opposite: Real freedom means the ability to change. Real freedom means the ability to go home—back to the source of life, to a place very close to God. The leper, a habitual gossiper guilty of excessive speech who is forced to leave his home, to exist in isolation, separated from society and from the holiness of the Temple, is capable of change—change that sets him free and allows him to reconnect with family and community, with man and God. Only then does he become truly free, and, like the freebird of the Psalms, he can go home—physically and spiritually.

---

27. Songwriters: Ronnie Van Zant and Allen Collins. Freebird lyrics © Universal Music Publishing Group.

Parshiyot
Aharei Mot–Kedoshim
A Nation of Priests

From the beginning of the book of *Vayikra*, our attention has been focused on the Mishkan and the rituals to be performed in it. When viewed as a corpus, the myriad laws that comprise "Leviticus" up to this point establish the Mishkan as the epicenter of the Jewish People—both in the geographical sense, as it was positioned in the encampment in the desert, and, as a result, in the symbolic sense, as the center of Jewish life. The various instances of *tumah* (usually translated as "impurity") enumerated in *Vayikra* are expressions of this Mishkan-centric reality. *Tumah* and the Mishkan are irreconcilable, and when an individual becomes impure, a process that restores him or her to a state of *taharah* (purity) is required before reentry into the Mishkan is once again possible.

Aharei Mot begins with the service to be performed each year on Yom Kippur. Even today, we are well-acquainted with the meaning of this day and its detailed ritual of atonement: On Yom Kippur, the *Kohen Gadol* follows the instructions laid out in *Parashat Aharei Mot* in order to heal the relationship between man and God. However, a careful reading reveals that although Yom Kippur focuses on expunging the sins accrued by the Jewish People over the course of the year, it is equally concerned with atoning for the sin of allowing the Mishkan itself to become impure.

This dual focus might lead us to the conclusion that the laws of purity and impurity enumerated in *Vayikra* are pertinent only insofar as the Mishkan is concerned—an orientation reflected in the moniker "Leviticus"—while outside the Mishkan, holiness was less important, if not altogether irrelevant.

The second section of *Parashat Aharei Mot* proves otherwise.

Following the discussion of the Yom Kippur service, *Aharei Mot* focuses on forbidden sexual liaisons. The shift in focus is abrupt, and it is significant for a number of reasons: First and foremost, orgiastic celebrations and other sexually depraved practices were common elements of ancient "religious" cultic practice. By creating clear, immutable categories of permitted and forbidden relationships, the Torah severely curtailed sexual behavior, making cultic licentiousness impossible.

However, the significance of these laws goes beyond the creation of new norms for religious expression. The laws enumerated in *Parashat Aharei Mot* go beyond the confines of the Mishkan; these are not exclusively "Temple" laws that regulate cultic practice. The prohibitions against sexual depravity were not only a consideration "before God" in the Mishkan or, later, in the Temple; these laws go far beyond eschewing the cultic and fertility rites common in the ancient world. These same norms, we are taught, apply to each and every one of us, in each and every home, each and every relationship and interaction. Here, then, lies the greater message: *Tumah* and *taharah* are

127

as applicable in the Temple as they are outside of the Temple. The Jewish home is a place of holiness; adultery, incest, and bestiality are unacceptable anywhere and everywhere.

From the moment they stood at the foot of Mount Sinai and prepared themselves to receive and obey Torah law, the Jewish People became not only a "treasured nation" and a "holy nation," but also a "kingdom of priests" (*Shemot* 19:5-6). This is no simple turn of phrase; it indicates that the entire People—men, women, and children—all have the status of priests (*kohanim*) at all times, in their normal lives, and not because they perform specific rituals in the Temple. To be sure, the rituals described in Leviticus could be performed only in the Mishkan (and, later, in the Temple in Jerusalem), but the laws of *tumah* and *taharah* were not limited to the Temple. The Jewish People were given laws of purity that would create holiness in their personal lives as well, and each and every Jewish home was imbued with this holiness. Each and every home became a sort of temple, and just as pagan sexual practices were not permitted in the Mishkan, so, too, these practices are forbidden in every home, assuring that the entire nation is holy—every person, in every locale, truly God's "treasured nation"—"a kingdom of priests."

Parashat Emor
Teach Your Children

Written upon the passing of Rabbi Dr. Aharon Lichtenstein, *zt"l*

As is often the case, the name of this week's *parashah* is taken from a word in the very first verse: *emor*, "speak." In fact, the act of speech appears three times in this verse:

> And God **said** to Moshe: **Speak** to the *kohanim*, the sons of Aharon, and **say** to them: Let none [of you] defile himself for a dead person among his people. (*Vayikra* 21:1)

The double "speak" is strange: The verse is unremarkable when it states that God spoke to Moshe; this is one of the more common formulations in the Torah, one we have come to expect. But the next two uses of the verb *emor* in this verse—translated here as "speak" and "say"—create a cumbersome textual passage that is uncharacteristic.

One possible understanding of this textual quirk is that the Torah's language creates an emphasis that might otherwise have been absent. By doubling the use of the verb, perhaps the message is that Moshe is charged with speaking to the *kohanim* in a way that will be heard, so that the message is understood, internalized and integrated.

Rashi offers an alternative explanation of this singular text. In his comments on this verse, he paraphrases a Talmudic passage that quotes this verse in a discussion regarding adults' responsibilities toward children (*Yevamot* 114a):

"Say [to the *kohanim*] and say [to them]," [This double expression comes] to warn [*lehazhir*] adults regarding minors. (Rashi, *Vayikra* 21:1)

When taken at face value, Rashi's comments on this verse contain an uplifting message: Not only should adults take responsibility for themselves, they should invest in the next generation and guide the young and innocent away from sin. We might easily use this teaching as a springboard for a broader discussion concerning the importance of positive, proactive education and the need to take responsibility for the next generation. Such would be the thrust of the message of our verse—unless we actually consulted with the Talmudic text upon which Rashi based his comments.

In fact, the Talmudic discussion actually contends with a far more ominous topic: Our verse is quoted in a passage that analyzes a number of cases in which an adult may be tempted to actually cause a child to sin. Far from an innocuous or even uplifting discussion of the virtues of religious education, the Talmudic passage contends with cases in which adults actively and purposefully lead children to astray! As opposed to the lofty world of educational responsibility and values we thought we had discerned in Rashi's comments on our verse, the Talmud forces us to confront the loathsome case of an adult introducing a child to sin.

We may attempt to understand the mindset of the adults in the Talmudic cases and to rationalize their behavior: Perhaps the cases involve young children, not yet at the age of bar- or bat-mitzvah, who are not legally responsible or culpable for their actions. For example, when there is a limited amount of kosher food available, an adult might conclude that the best option would be to eat the kosher food and give the underage child something non-kosher.

This scenario inevitably leads to a more abstract, even philosophical discussion about the very nature of sin and its impact on the human being. Is sin merely a question of culpability? If the transgression is not punishable, is it of any significance? In more colloquial terms, can we say that sin is akin to the proverbial tree that falls in the forest; if there is no one to punish, does the sin make a sound, as it were, or does sin affect the soul, leaving a mark or stain that is independent of culpability? The Talmudic passage in question seems to extrapolate an additional, even more far-reaching lesson from our verse: Causing someone to sin is akin to feeding them spiritual poison, and this behavior stains the soul of the instigator as well as the perpetrator—particularly when the transgression is committed by a young, unsuspecting and impressionable soul.

The conclusion we are forced to draw from a careful reading of Rashi's Talmudic source is that the first verse in *Parashat Emor* teaches responsibility: not, as we originally thought, that

A Taste of Eden

we must educate the next generation, but as a warning against corrupting the next generation and causing our children to sin. This message is far more poignant and perhaps more difficult to fulfill. Certainly, we teach our children to do good things and to avoid things that are religiously distasteful. The question is, do we transmit messages akin to "Do as I say, not as I do"? Are we somehow corrupting the next generation, causing them to sin through unspoken, non-verbal messages, and by setting a poor example?

In Rashi's comments on the verse, he uses the term *gedolim*, which we have translated as "adults"; this same term is also used colloquially to describe our great rabbis. The *gedolim* have responsibility for the *ketanim*, those who are underage or of lesser stature and learning. This past week we lost one of our *gedolim*, Rabbi Dr. Aharon Lichtenstein, may his righteous memory be a blessing. I, along with tens of thousands of his students, can attest that Rav Aharon not only educated us, he "took care" of us spiritually. He was a living, breathing model of *ahavat Torah*, love of Torah learning and devout observance, as well as *yirat Shamayim*, God-fearing awe and respect for holiness. He shared with us his vision and served as a model for proper behavior, setting a very high benchmark for all Jews in the modern world—and he did all this with love, dedication, eloquence, humility and nobility. For this we will be forever indebted, and express our enduring thanks and love.

Parashat B'Har
Dayenu!

Modern colloquial Hebrew uses an ancient rabbinicism when asking what two seemingly disparate subjects have to do with one another. The phrase, drawn from comments on the first verse of *Parashat B'Har*, is: "What does *shemittah* have to do with Mount Sinai?"

This week's Torah reading begins with what seems to be superfluous information: "God spoke to Moshe at Mount Sinai, saying..." In fact, every single communication in the thirty chapters preceding this *parashah* occurred at Mount Sinai, starting with Chapter 19 in the Book of *Shemot*. Why, then, does this geographic place-marker appear specifically in this chapter, which deals with the laws of the sabbatical and Jubilee years? What, indeed, is the connection between *shemittah* and Mount Sinai?

When the Jews arrived at Mount Sinai they were nothing more than a ragtag group of former slaves, dazed by the wonders they had seen but broken in spirit by hundreds of years of servitude and abuse. They knew that they were, in effect, an extended family, descendants of the twelve sons of Israel, but when they arrived at Sinai, something magical happened: They became united, and came to realize that in addition to their shared history, they have a shared destiny. At the foot of Mount Sinai, they accepted the challenge of that shared destiny, and expressed their willingness to accept the Torah, the means through which that destiny would be brought to fruition.

It is that magical moment of realization and comprehension that is celebrated in the words we sing at the Seder on Pesach: "Had God brought us to Mount Sinai and not given us the Torah, it would have been sufficient"—*Dayenu*! The Sinai experience was not solely a question of receiving the Torah. Receiving the Law, the charter for this newly emerging nation, was only possible after the people assembled at the foot of the mountain realized that they were in the process of becoming a covenantal community that would create an enlightened, spiritual society that would change the world. The Revelation at Sinai was predicated by this experience of unity, of acknowledging their shared history and accepting the mantle of their shared destiny. Had they achieved only this at the foot of Sinai—unity of purpose and mutual responsibility for their destiny—it would have sufficed.

The laws of *shemittah* (sabbatical) and *yovel* (Jubilee) create unity. Every seven years the farmer is reminded that the land does not ultimately belong to him; it is the property of God. The farmer is commanded to let the land lie fallow, and all its produce becomes ownerless. We are all forced to reconsider the basic concepts of ownership and property; in the seventh year, everything that grows in the Land of Israel belongs to every Jew equally; more accurately—it belongs to God, and He forces us to share it in the seventh year. The mighty, wealthy landowner and the poor, unemployed or itinerant worker have equal claim to the produce of the *shemittah* year. Social strata and divisions are broken down, and the core of unity that lies at the heart of Jewish nationhood rises to the surface. *Shemittah* forces us to reconnect with the unity we first found at the foot of Mount Sinai.

In modern times, *shemittah* observance is quite a challenge. My late great teacher Rabbi Aharon Lichtenstein lamented[28] that there really is no ideal "solution" in the modern state that satisfies all the halachic and social principles of *shemittah* observance. One approach sees the national economy or the welfare of Israeli farmers as the major concern, while another approach subordinates these concerns, despite the fact that preferring non-Jewish produce may directly support those who pose a threat to the security of the Jewish State.

The result of these divergent and often opposing approaches to the laws of *shemittah* results in a situation that runs counter to the very spirit of *shemittah:* Religious Jews who would otherwise dine at one another's tables and take part in one another's celebrations refrain from these most basic expressions of unity and community during the *shemittah* year. The situation is further exacerbated by sincere Jews and *kashrut* organizations around the world whose scrupulous observance of their interpretation of the laws of *shemittah* leads them to unwittingly participate in a boycott of Jewish produce for the duration of the *shemittah* year (and a significant period thereafter)—a boycott instigated by the greatest of Israel's enemies.

To be clear: the sincerity or validity of these positions are beyond question, and I personally would not dream of standing

---

28. See Rabbi Aharon Lichtenstein "Thoughts about Shemittah," *Leaves of Faith*, volume 2 (2004), pp. 179-188; "Reflections on Shemitta," 5761, VBM Sichot; "The Dilemma of Shemitta Today," *Alei Etzion* 15 (2007), pp. 15-21.

A Taste of Eden

in judgment of those who follow the opinions of the various rabbinic authorities who support the divergent resolutions of the modern *shemittah* quandary. On the other hand, the lesson of this week's Torah reading should not be disregarded: "What does *shemittah* have to do with Mount Sinai?" At the foot of Mount Sinai, we stood as one—with one heart, a people united by history and destiny, intensely aware of our mutual responsibility—and now, every seven years, with the onset of *shemittah*, we become a people divided. "What does *shemittah* have to do with Mount Sinai?" These days, apparently very little indeed.

Parashat Bechukotai
There's No Place Like Home

Unfortunately, sometimes relationships deteriorate, and when they do, each side has thoughts about the wisdom of continuing, of staying together. Is the heartache worth it? Is the emotional cost justifiable?

What if the relationship in question is between God and His Chosen People? What happens when that relationship deteriorates? If they have a "trial separation," what would it take for both sides to give the relationship a second chance?

Looking back at the episodes and events recorded in the Torah from the Exodus to this point, we realize that there were many "cracks in the ice"; the love story that had begun on such a promising note was not really on solid ground. God, of course was fully aware, from the outset, that the "honeymoon" would eventually come to an end: The redemption from Egypt, which is likened to a knight in shining armor swooping in to rescue a damsel in distress,[29] would be eclipsed by duplicity and faithlessness on the part of the Jewish People.

Parashat Bechukotai spells out the details of estrangement: The bond, the covenant sealed at Sinai, is broken. As a result,

---

29. *Yirmiyahu* 2:2.

we become homeless and alone. The Land of Israel is no longer ours, and we are cast into exile.

How can this broken relationship be repaired? What is needed to bring about reconciliation? How can we become worthy of the love and trust we violated? What can we do to deserve to come back home? The verse that describes the process of reconciliation is somewhat enigmatic:

I will remember My covenant with Yaakov as well as My covenant with Yitzchak and My covenant with Avraham and I will remember the Land. (*Vayikra* 26:42)

It strikes us that this verse is written in inverse order; the normal sequence begins with Avraham and ends with Yaakov. Additionally, the verse speaks of God "remembering" the Land. This seems to contradict the very foundations of our belief in God who exists beyond the constraints of time and space: God does not "forget," nor does He need to be reminded. We repeat this very basic tenet of faith over and over in the liturgy of the High Holy Days: "For there is no forgetting in front of God's throne."

In fact, the impetus for reconciliation, what "causes" God to remember, as it were, is our own "remembering"—what Jewish mysticism calls "an awakening from below." Man stirs; the Jewish People remember where they should be and become acutely aware of what they have lost through their infidelity, and reach out to God from the exile. This awakening, this human gesture of remorse that seeks to rekindle lost intimacy, triggers God's response, the "awakening from above."

Parashat Bechukotai

But what of the strange sequence of the verse? Why are the patriarchs "remembered" in inverse order? It seems that this verse lays out the mechanics, the method, the specific steps that must be taken to restore the relationship, by presenting the three forefathers as representatives of three distinct modes of serving God:[30] Yaakov represents Torah study and observance (he was a man of study who "dwelled in tents"[31]). Yitzchak represents *avodah* (ritual service, sacrifice and complete submission of the kind he displayed when he was placed upon the altar[32]). Avraham represents *chesed*, kindness.

The covenant that allows the Jewish People to live in peace and intimacy with God in the Land of Israel was forged on the basis of their acceptance of the Torah. For reconciliation to take place, they must recommit themselves to Torah. In order to renew the covenant, they must fulfill the original terms of the covenant. For this reason, Yaakov is mentioned before the other patriarchs.

What if this is too tall an order for us? What if a generation emerges that is estranged from Torah observance? Is reconciliation still possible? The verse does not end with the covenant of Yaakov; in His infinite mercy, God does not hold us to that standard. He does not demand that we live up to the terms of that covenant in order to rekindle our relationship with Him. He is willing to accept a rekindling of the covenant of Yitzchak: If we turn to him in prayer, if we are willing to

---

30. I heard this idea from Rabbi Isaac Bernstein, but he could not recall where he originally heard it. See *Torah Yesharah* by Rabbi Chas. Kahane, vol. 2, p. 211 (this reference was pointed out to me by Zacharyah T. Honikman).
31. *Bereishit* 25:27, understood by the rabbis to be the "tents of Torah study."
32. *Bereishit* 22:9.

submit our ego and wholeheartedly serve God, we may still merit reconciliation.

What if our generation is devoid of the basic consciousness of God expressed by Torah observance, Torah study, even of prayer? The verse in *Parashat Bechukotai* indicates that as long as we practice kindness, if we are scrupulous in our interpersonal relationships and comportment like Avraham, we will still be able to come home.

And what if even this decency and mutual responsibility is lost? Is reconciliation still possible? Is there any way to end our exile and estrangement? The conclusion of this verse holds out one last hope: "I will remember the Land." If a sincere and potent "remembering of the Land" arises from below—even if it is devoid of the other three components—reconciliation is still possible.

The implication is clear: There is no need for identical perspectives or total agreement on all issues in order to create, maintain, rekindle or repair a relationship; one passionately shared element is enough.

Recent history has seen hundreds of thousands of Jews return to the Land of Israel, in what can only be called a reawakening of the Jewish spirit. This alone is sufficient to stir the awakening above. Now, to solidify the relationship, we must move to the next stage in our covenantal history. Like Avraham, we must build our environment—beginning with our personal relationships, our households, our communities and our nation—on *chesed*. We must rediscover our voice, and pray to God in earnest, like Yitzchak. And we must find our way back to real Torah learning and observance—and completely live up to our side of the covenant.

Parashat Bechukotai

Until we are able to collectively achieve these goals, though, it is nice to know that God is willing to welcome us home simply because we really want to come back home.

Parashat Bemidbar
The Theory of Conservation of Holiness

As the Book of *Bemidbar* begins, the Israelites have been encamped at the foot of Sinai for over a year, and we begin to sense a stirring that will soon become forward movement: First, instructions are given for conducting a census, followed by demarcation of marching formations and tribal flags. The mass of people who took leave of Egypt is organized according to tribal affiliation, and the tribes are grouped into *mahanot* (camps) as they begin preparations for the second part of their march, from Sinai to the Promised Land.

One tribe, however, is not included in any of these preparatory steps: the Levites are neither counted in the census nor included in the marching formation. The Levites, unique among the tribes, have no flag or standard around which they gather. They are a tribe with a singular mandate, designated to serve in the Mishkan; they belong to God.

This had not always been the case; until a certain point in time, the tribe of Levi had been like any of the other tribes, equal in every way to the other eleven. Moreover, the unique designation of dedicated service to God had not previously been the purview of any one tribe. Originally, the firstborn of each and every Israelite family was dedicated to Divine service. What happened? Why were the firstborn displaced and replaced by the Levites? The Torah does not provide a clear answer:

> God spoke to Moshe, saying: I have separated the Levites from the children of Israel, so that they may take the place of all the firstborn among the Israelites, and the Levites shall be Mine. This is because every firstborn became Mine on the day I killed all the firstborn in Egypt. I then sanctified to Myself every firstborn in Israel, man and beast alike, [and] they shall remain Mine. I am God. (*Bemidbar* 3:11-13)

This passage explains how and why the firstborn were initially sanctified with a special holiness: On the night all the firstborn were killed in Egypt, the firstborn of the Israelites were spared. Apparently, this was neither arbitrary nor without repercussions: The Israelite firstborn were saved for a purpose, to serve God in the Temple, and because they were saved they were granted a higher status of holiness. Why was this holiness forfeited? When were the firstborn replaced by the Levites?

On two different occasions, the firstborn sons were given the opportunity to carry out their unique role. These two occasions were very different from one another, both in circumstance and in their implications and ramifications: The first opportunity that arose was at the foot of Mount Sinai, as the people prepared for the Revelation. Offerings were brought,[33] and it is presumed that the firstborn served as religious functionaries

---

33. *Shemot* 24:5.

for the exalted religious experience that prepared the people for what was to follow. The next "opportunity" presented itself some forty days later, when Moshe was nowhere to be seen and the situation began to spiral out of control: A golden calf was formed and the people brought offerings and worshipped the icon they had created.[34] Once again, the firstborn acted as *kohanim*, preparing and offering the sacrilegious sacrifices and leading the way for the nation as a whole. In so doing, the firstborn forfeited their place as *kohanim*, and were replaced by the "first responders," the Levites who answered Moshe's call to arms and quashed the rebellion.

Interestingly, the holiness that had belonged to the firstborn did not simply dissipate when they forfeited their unique role. There is, it seems, a "theory of conservation of holiness": Holiness is neither created nor destroyed by human behavior. The source of holiness is God, and when the subject upon which holiness is bestowed becomes unable or unworthy to maintain the required level of proximity to God, the holiness is transferred to a different subject. Thus, after the firstborn strayed, the Levites, who stood passionately in defense of God and real holiness and eschewed the golden imposter, were endowed with the holiness wrested from the firstborn in an act of transference.

On the other hand, despite the shift of their special role to the Levites, the firstborn retained a vestige of their previous holiness; despite the relative spiritual estrangement, holiness does not disappear. From that point, both the firstborn and the Levites are endowed with holiness, even though only the Levites can serve in the Temple. The holiness of the firstborn, the spiritual glow of serving God at Sinai, is never erased,

34. *Shemot* 32:6.

even though Temple service is no longer an option. From that time forth, the firstborn of all non-Levites must be redeemed, released from the obligation of service for which they are no longer worthy.

Such is holiness: it does not disappear. Tasks and responsibilities may be reassigned to others, but the holiness of the firstborn is retained. Perhaps this idea holds out hope for the entire Jewish People: The moment they worshipped the golden calf, in violation of the covenant they had made with God only days earlier, God could have turned His back on them entirely, for they had proven themselves unworthy of the holy destiny to which God had appointed them. And yet, we continue to be God's Chosen People, "a kingdom of priests and a holy nation." The holiness with which we were imbued at Mount Sinai is everlasting. Its source is God Himself, and therefore it, too, is eternal.

Parashat Naso
The Sin of Asceticism

There are times in a person's life that holiness becomes a conscious goal, a state of mind and body that he or she actively pursues, a desideratum. However, the quest to achieve a higher plane of existence, to attain spiritual elevation, is not always a simple or straightforward path. The desire for spirituality can lead us along strange and uncharted roads, at times taking us in a direction or to a place which is either devoid of holiness or, even worse, the antithesis of holiness. Numerous sections of the Torah and the majority of the words of the prophets are dedicated to the seemingly never-ending battle against false pagan gods whose seductive promise of a quick "one night stand" of ecstatic religious experience leads unsuspecting seekers astray. Sensuality, sexuality, sensory overload and artificially altered states of consciousness have long served as key "marketing tools" for the false nirvana offered by paganism in its various forms—from the dawn of time to the present.

The truly sensitive soul eschews spiritual counterfeits, and seeks holiness elsewhere—often in the very antithesis of the debauchery and carnal excess that characterizes paganism. The Torah presents one such model, in which the spiritual seeker can achieve an altered state, an elevated level of holiness. In this model, a person can either temporarily or permanently step outside their normal existence and become a "different" person, taking on new, more restrictive limitations of their sensory and physical existence. In so doing, the spiritual seeker becomes a *nazir*.

Some of these additional restrictions are reminiscent of the laws that apply to a *kohen*, and even a *kohen gadol*, such as the prohibition against voluntary contact with the dead, even close relatives. Similarly, wine is forbidden to the *nazir*, as it is to a *kohen* during his period of active service in the Temple. Although these parallels might lead us to equate the *nazir* and the *kohen*, there is one major difference, perhaps designed to remind the *nazir* that he is not a *kohen*: the *nazir*'s hair must be left uncut, whereas the *kohen gadol* (high priest) is specifically commanded to be well-coiffed.[35]

The *nazir* might be deluded by the similarity with the lofty spiritual status of the *kohen*, and draw inappropriate conclusions. However, one additional law regarding the *nazir* must be taken into account. Surprisingly, the Torah commands the *nazir* to bring a sin offering to the Temple when the assigned period is completed and normal life is resumed. Upon reflection, this seems quite strange: The *nazir* has just completed a period of heightened spirituality, of asceticism and self-denial, of abstention from various aspects of the physical world. Why would a sin offering be appropriate at the end of this period of holiness?

The nature of this sin offering is debated in the Talmud. One opinion is that the sin offering is brought because the

---

35. *Vayikra* 21:10; compare with *Vayikra* 10:6.

A Taste of Eden

nazir may have unwittingly failed to live up to his new status at some point in the process. The other opinion is that the offering atones for the "sins" that are part and parcel of the nazirite experience itself—namely, abstinence from wine that would otherwise have been enjoyed. This teaching may come as a surprise; after all, Judaism does not usually concern itself with lamenting unfulfilled desires or earthly pleasures—but the Talmudic teaching[36] is quite clear: This world was made to be enjoyed, celebrated, and sanctified.

God created a beautiful world, and He placed the first man and woman in the "Garden of Eden" —quite literally, the garden of pleasure. In a particularly beautiful passage, the Talmud teaches that a person who fails to enjoy the beautiful world God gave us will be held accountable as he or she stands in judgment at the end of their life. The Talmud then recounts the custom of one particular sage who took this teaching to heart and made it his custom to visit the market regularly in the hope of finding some new fruit or other delicacy, seeking out new tastes in order to be able to recite the appropriate blessing and have an opportunity to say the "*shehecheyanu*," to appreciate the wonder and variety of God's creation and to avoid the wrath of Heaven should he fail to take advantage of all that God created for the pleasure and benefit of mankind.[37]

The *nazir's* decision to take on a level of asceticism, to forego certain earthly pleasures, is an option that the Torah condones for those who feel they are in need of more sharply-defined boundaries in order to achieve a higher level of spirituality. However, this decision has consequences: The *nazir* has taken

---

36. *Ta'anit* 11a.
37. Jerusalem Talmud, *Kiddushin* 4:12.

Parashat Naso

a vow that precludes taking full enjoyment from the physical world, and for this, the *nazir* must make amends. As he (or she) prepares to return to his former life, he must "apologize" to God for passing up on the pleasures this world has to offer. The *nazir*'s sin-offering, then, is an important message for us all: In His benevolence, God created a world of wonder and delight, which He allows us to share. The Torah is the framework through which the pleasures of this world can be experienced and appreciated, enjoyed—and sanctified.

Parashat BeHaalotcha
The Seven Books

One God, two Tablets, three patriarchs, four matriarchs, and five books of the Torah; that is how the song from the Haggadah goes, as every Jewish child knows.

The corpus of our Written Law has long been identified as the Five Books of Moshe, the Chumash (derived from the Hebrew word *chamesh*, meaning five) or Pentateuch, which also denotes that it is comprised of five books. This is clear, self-evident and indisputable—or is it?

Rabbinic tradition may be far less unequivocal: for example, Rashi's comments on the verse, "[Wisdom] has hewn out her seven pillars"[38]: Rashi explains that the seven pillars are the "seven books of the Torah,"[39] despite the fact that the last time any of us looked, there were five books, no more and no less. Rashi's cryptic comment reflects an earlier tradition that the book of *Bemidbar* is actually made of three separate books: The first begins with *Bemidbar* 1:1 and ends at 10:34. The third

---

38. *Mishlei* 9:1.
39. I was first introduced to this concept, which is based on comments of the Seforno on *Bemidbar* 10:35-36, by my father, who in turn heard it from Rabbi Yosef Soloveitchik in a lecture entitled *Nos'im Anachnu*. (Rabbi Soloveitchik's lecture on this topic can be on the yutorah.org website.)

book begins with *Bemidbar* 11:1 and continues through the last verse of what we know as the book of *Bemidbar.* The material between these two "books" is the second book, to which we will return momentarily; first, let us examine the first and last of these three books.

The contrast between the two is stark: The former is a book of hope and purpose, as the Israelites prepare to take their first steps of departure from Sinai. The latter is a book of missteps, as the Israelites flounder from one debacle to the next, getting no closer to their destination. This might be an exaggeration—at the end of the book the Jews stand at the cusp of the Promised Land—but not much: forty years pass and the Promised Land remains an elusive destination, an unfulfilled promise.

All this leads us back to the second book that comprises *Bemidbar,* which is the strangest one of all. This book consists of only two verses, a mere 85 letters (in Hebrew):[40]

When the Ark traveled, Moshe said, "Arise, God! Scatter Your enemies, and let those who hate You flee before You." And when the Ark rested, he would say, "Return, God, the myriad of thousands of Israel!" (10: 35-36)

How can two verses be considered a book? And why are these two specific verses given this distinction? To make matters even more inscrutable, these verses are actually set apart visually from all other verses in the Torah, enclosed within a unique set of "brackets" or parentheses that are not used anywhere else: a pair of symbols created by what look like the inverted Hebrew

---

40. See Mishnah, *Yadayim* 3:5; *Bereishit Rabbah* 64:8; *Vayikra Rabbah* 11:3; *Talmud Bavli Shabbat* 115b-116a. For more on this topic, see "Parashat Beha'alotcha: The Unfinished Book" in *Explorations,* pp. 325ff.

letter *noon*. This book-within-a-book, only two verses long, is distinguished from everything that comes before and after it, alerting us to the fact that here is something quite extraordinary. These are not simply a pair of innocuous verses; they indicate that something monumental happened, or to be more accurate, that something monumental did *not* happen—and therein lies the key to this unique, truncated book.

What do these two verses actually tell us? The Holy Ark of the Covenant moves, for the first time since its creation, and Moshe calls out to God to scatter His enemies. What enemies are these? Quite simply, the nations occupying the Land of Israel: The time had come for the Israelites to come home and reclaim their birthright. However, this explanation raises even more questions than it answers: What became of this triumphant march? As we know, Moshe never did spearhead the conquest of the Land of Israel; tragically, he died too soon and was not allowed to cross the Jordan. In a nutshell, this ephemeral second book within *Bemidbar* tells the story of what should have been.

As *Bemidbar* opens, the Jews make the necessary preparations to leave Mount Sinai and march to Israel. The third book recounts their wanderings and rebellions, covering the next 39 years. This middle book leaves a remnant of what *should* have taken place at that specific juncture. Armed with the Torah, unified as a nation with a glorious mission to fulfill, all that remained was to complete their short victory march. Instead, they make one foolish mistake after another; the vision encapsulated in these two verses does not come to fruition in Moshe's lifetime.

In essence, we may say that the Torah might have ended at this moment in history: The covenant between God and

Parashat BeHaalotcha

Avraham would be realized as the Ark of the Covenant led them into the land of their fathers. The two strange verses that comprise this second book are a remnant of the book that was not written, the story that is never told, the alternative ending, the road not taken. In a manner that is never repeated, the Torah records what *should* have happened: First, the glorious march to the Land of Israel led by Moshe and the Ark of the Covenant:

> When the Ark traveled, Moshe said, "Arise, God! Scatter Your enemies, and let those who hate You flee before You."

Then, the final chord:

> "Return, God, the myriad of thousands of Israel!"

These two short, idyllic statements are the first and last verses of an uncompleted book, an account of events that never happened. The first verse describes the march to Israel led by Moshe—a march that would have been a bloodless conquest, devoid of conflict, as the tribes that had taken up residence in the Land of Israel would have "exited, stage left." The second verse describes the culmination of history, when the Ark finally reaches its permanent resting place.

Tragically, all that remains of this idyllic denouement are the first and last verses, the hint of what should have been— and, perhaps, of what might yet be: When we are able to retake that moment in history, to climb back up to that level of preparedness that will allow us to pick up the narrative of the second book, we will be able to complete the triumphant tale. God will see to it that our enemies are vanquished, and all the Jews lost throughout the millennia of our seemingly aimless wandering will return home. As that final scene begins, a voice will call out:

"Return, God, the myriad of thousands of Israel!"

The ingathering of the Jewish exiles and the return of the Ark to its rightful place in Jerusalem were meant to be—and, one day, will be—the completion of the book of Jewish history, the book hinted at by these two verses in *Parashat BeHaalotcha*. This is the book of our potential, of our as-yet-unfulfilled destiny. May we merit its completion, speedily and in our days.

Parashat Sh'lach
A Divine Rendezvous

Group dynamics are interesting and complex. Individuals who come from different places, geographically or emotionally, see the same situation in different ways. In the episode of the so-called spies, this phenomenon repeats itself over and over.

The first instance may be seen in the divergent reports delivered by the twelve emissaries who are sent to scout the Land of Israel. Ten of the scouts speak of the Land's beauty and bounty, but stress that conquest is not a viable option. The eleventh man, Calev (Caleb), insists that the land is conquerable, while the twelfth scout, Yehoshua (Joshua), remains silent. Remarkably, God is not a factor in the discussion: Divine intervention and the supernatural protection they continue to enjoy are not taken into consideration by any of the opposing sides in the debate.

Calev is adamant, and refuses to fall in line with the majority, which leads the ten dissidents to change tactics: Making a subtle shift, they malign the Land itself and cast its desirability into question. Fear leads to mass hysteria; panic sets in. Suddenly, life and death as slaves seem preferable to the uncertain future that awaits them in the Promised Land (14:2), and the masses begin to plot overthrowing their leaders and returning to Egypt

(14:4). It is likely that this consequence, the rebellion against Moshe and Aharon, was neither intended nor anticipated by the spies: They themselves were tribal leaders, and would likely have been cast aside in the same putsch.

Calev and Yehoshua protest: If God wills it, the conquest will happen. The Land, they insist, is exceedingly good. Here, then, are two different perspectives on the same set of observations: Is the Land conquerable? Is it desirable? What should the next stage of their collective history look like? One opinion, championed by Calev, is to forge ahead and begin the conquest; the masses prefer to abort the entire project and return to Egypt. A third group emerges: the very same people who started the debate, the ten spies who opined that going forward was not an option yet did not articulate an alternative plan of action, stand bewildered, even dumbfounded.

At this point, God intervenes. He threatens to eradicate the entire people and build a new nation from Moshe's descendants, but Moshe intercedes, pleading and praying, until a drastically reduced sentence is handed down: The malicious spies perish in a plague, and the masses who preferred Egypt or even death in the wilderness are banned from entering the Land they had rejected. In an ironic twist of poetic justice, they are doomed to die in the desert; only their children will merit entrance to the Land. Of the entire generation that left Egypt, Yehoshua and Calev would be the sole survivors.

In the aftermath of this tragic series of events, something strange happens. Another group forms, a group whose identity or size are not revealed. They reject the punishment, the death sentence that hangs over them, and decide that the time is ripe to conquer the Land of Israel. Tragically, they are massacred in battle.

Parashat Sh'lach

Who were the members of this ill-advised group of would-be warriors? The Torah provides no details; all that is left to us is conjecture. While we might be tempted to say that the ten rogue spies repented and sought to correct the damage they had done, this is not an option: The text clearly states that they were already dead. One other certainty is that neither Calev nor Yehoshua were party to this effort; they both lived to fight another day.

While the possibilities seem endless, we can nonetheless narrow down the field of candidates. It seems unlikely that those who were so terrified of war that they preferred slavery and certain death, were suddenly emboldened. Only two reasonable candidates remain: the tribes of Calev and Yehoshua, the two dissenting scouts: Yehuda and Efraim.

While both are excellent candidates, one tribe in particular has fidelity to the Land of Israel indelibly imprinted in its spiritual DNA. While Calev's enthusiastic "Yes we can" (13:30) response to the spies' disheartening assessment is certainly impressive, it seems far more likely that descendants of Yosef would take up the cause of Eretz Yisrael:[41] Yehoshua was a descendant of Efraim, the son of Yosef—the same Yosef who mourned his personal exile, and whose dying wish was that he be carried out of Egypt and buried in Israel. Generations later, the daughters of Zelafhad[42] from the tribe of Menashe, Yosef's elder son, were unwilling to forfeit their inheritance in the Land of Israel. Time and again, the children of Yosef express a greater yearning for the Land of Israel. Yehoshua's own tribe seems

41. *Sifri, Bemidbar* 133 states that the descendants of Yosef had a particular love of the Land of Israel.
42. The Talmud (*Shabbat* 96a) suggests that Zlafhad may have been one of those who died on this failed mission.

likely to have spearheaded the push to conquer the Land; just as the head of the tribe, Yehoshua, would one day lead the battle, they decide to step forward.

Unfortunately, they seem to have failed to internalize the thrust of Yehoshua's message: The conquest will take place when God wills it, and only when He is in their midst. They had taken the wrong message from the sin of the spies, concluding that the time had come, and that they could correct the error of those who had eschewed the land by actively taking their future into their own hands. A comparison of census data before and after this episode reveals that the tribe of Ephraim suffered a sudden, drastic drop in population.[43] Apparently, in a tragic mix of bravery, self-confidence and misguided idealism, this band of Efraimites, known as the *Ma'apilim*, thought they could force God's hand, as it were. Perhaps they hoped to "catch up" with their destiny, which they saw slipping away. They must have hoped to reconcile with God in the Land of Israel, but they did not think they needed His help to get there.

Once again, we are struck by the difference in perspective: Ten spies considered God uninvolved, and did not figure Him into the equation at all. The masses thought that God hated them (*Devarim* 1:27) and fully expected to be eradicated. The *Ma'apilim* looked forward to meeting God at the end of the battle, in an intimate rendezvous in The Land of Israel. Only Yehoshua and Calev fully understood that the only way to enter the Land is *with* God.

The message should not be lost on us: Although the events of modern history may also be interpreted from many different perspectives, there is, in fact, one interpretation that

---

43. As noted by the Radak in his commentary 1 Chronicles 7:21.

Parashat Sh'lach

is more correct, more relevant, than the others: The miraculous ingathering of the exiles we are witnessing in the modern era is nothing short of the hand of God bringing His People back home for that great, long-awaited rendezvous.

Parashat Korach
A Jealous Guy

There was once a man who was blessed in many ways: he was smart, he was wealthy and he came from a very good family. His name was Korach. From the outside it looked like he had everything going for him, but something went wrong: there was a tragic malfunction and his beautiful life crumbled.

Korach was a Levite, a blood relative of Moshe and Aharon and related to Nahshon by marriage—all significant leaders, each in his own right and in his own sphere; Korach was not. There was a time, when he was a young man, that things looked brighter for him: As a firstborn son, he was assured a position of service in the Temple—a position of exalted status and respect. But in the aftermath of the sin of the golden calf, the firstborn sons, who had participated in the sin, were replaced by the tribe of Levi.

And here was the irony: Korach's cousin Aharon, who also hailed from the tribe of Levi, was arguably the *only* member of the tribe who was guilty of complicity in the golden calf debacle. In fact, it was the Levites—Korach's and Aharon's extended family—who "cleaned up the mess" and rid the world of those who had been active participants in that terrible sin. Why, then, was Korach "downgraded" from the position of *kohen* that was the birthright of the firstborn, and reduced to the status of "generic" Levite, while Aharon, whose hands were far from clean of sin, was awarded the supreme position of *Kohen Gadol*? Such was Korach's view of the events, and the situation did not sit well with him.

And if this were not enough to raise Korach's hackles, he did not need to look further than the next major sin committed in the desert, the sin of the spies. The Levites had not sent a representative to scout the land. The only member of their tribe who was involved in this sin, who had any level of complicity whatsoever, was Moshe, the man who had sent the spies on their mission in the first place.

The tribe of Levi had no part in the two major sins committed by the Israelites in the desert—with two notable exceptions: Aharon played no small role in the creation of the golden calf, and Moshe was the catalyst that set the sin of the spies in motion. Korach was infuriated by what he perceived as the injustice of it all: He himself had been denied the position of service in the Temple that would now be taken by Aharon and his sons, while Moshe and Aharon seemed to be made of Teflon: The stain of these massive transgressions did not stick to them, and they slipped away unscathed. This may well be the background to Korach's rebellion: He was driven to distraction by what was, in his opinion, the unfairness of it all.

Jealousy can be a powerful, self-destructive force; for Korach, it gave rise to self-righteousness, which he focused on issues of holiness—that is, the holiness of every member of the community other than Moshe and Aharon. He was capable of seeing and appreciating his own holiness, and the holiness

A Taste of Eden

intrinsic in every Jew who stood at Mount Sinai, but the holiness of Moshe and Aharon escaped him. Another fact that seems to have slipped his jealousy-ravaged mind was the source of Moshe and Aharon's authority. Who, indeed, had appointed them to the lofty positions they held? Surely, Moshe had not actively sought out the spotlight. He had neither campaigned for the job nor sought exclusivity in his various roles as leader, judge or teacher; quite the opposite: God had to cajole Moshe to take up the reins of leadership, and Moshe repeatedly expressed his desire to share responsibility with the elders, even encouraging others who showed that they were capable of prophecy.

Leadership comes with a price. The people will inevitably err, and the leadership will inevitably be blamed. Real leadership is not measured by the ability to avoid all mistakes, but by the ability to minimize them, to foresee and forestall them whenever possible, and to confront the mistakes that will inevitably be made, not cover them up. Real leadership learns from past mistakes and tries to create systems and processes that will prevent their recurrence. There will always be people lying in wait on the sidelines, the slings and arrows of criticism in hand, poised to take advantage of any misstep in order to promote the implicit message that they themselves could do a better job. Blinded by ambition or jealousy, what they often fail to consider is the mistakes and tragedies that were avoided thanks to the strong and steady hand of the leadership they are so quick to criticize. From the comfort of their secure positions on the sidelines, they see only the flaws.

Korach had been handed one of the most important supporting roles in the Israelite camp: He and his family carried the Holy Ark when the Mishkan traveled. Yet rather

Parashat Korach

than embracing the sacred trust that had been placed in him, rather than reveling in the proximity he had been granted to what was literally the holiest thing on earth, Korach attacked the members of his own family: He wanted what they had.

Among the great gifts Korach had been given was his children. They were not tainted by their father's jealousy, and when their father rebelled, they sided with Moshe and Aharon. They were more than content with the task assigned to them; they felt honored to have been entrusted with carrying the Ark of the Covenant. When their father fell into the abyss, they did not go down with him. They lived on, fulfilling their sacred role, and their descendants in turn lived on to serve and sing in the Temple. Korach's descendants rose to the challenge of the task they had been assigned, and they brought honor to their service, which in turn brought them honor and distinction. They were holy people, from a holy family, whereas Korach lost everything: his honor, his wealth, the respect of his children, and his life. Such is the power of jealousy.

Parashat Chukat
Déjà Vu – All Over Again?

It seems like déjà vu: a lack of resources leads to complaints, which brings about Divine intercession—and so it goes, again and again. But this time is different. This time, instead of the people suffering for their impatience and insolence, it is Moshe and Aharon who are punished. Remarkably, they are accused of a lack of faith in God:

> God said to Moshe and Aharon, "You did not have enough faith in Me to sanctify Me in the presence of the Israelites! Therefore, you shall not bring this assembly to the land that I have given them." (20:12)

The punishment is sudden and shocking, but what was the transgression that brought the leadership of Moshe and Aharon to an end? How could they, of all people who ever lived, be accused of not believing in God?

By this point in the narrative, we are accustomed to the complaints—the lovely food they had in Egypt,[44] the wisdom of having gone off to die in the desert rather than staying put

---

44. *Shemot* 16:3; *Bemidbar* 11:4-5.

in Egypt, where there were ample graveyards.[45] The complaints were taken to a new level by Datan and Aviram, who accused Moshe of having taken them *from* a land that flowed with milk and honey![46] Moshe reacts to this latest round of complaining in much the same way as he did when the people first began their complaints years before.[47] The two instances seem so similar to us that we are not surprised when Moshe once again strikes the rock to draw out water, this time adding a verbal rebuke for good measure:

> "Listen now, you rebels!" shouted Moshe. "Shall we produce water for you from this rock?" (20:10)

In what seems to be an expression of frustration with the cumulative corpus of complaints and criticism, Moshe lumps the latest example of the peoples' dissatisfaction together with all the previous episodes, calling them rebels. And yet, despite the general sense that this litany of complaints has been heard over and over, there is something different in this particular case.

> The people did not have any water, so they began demonstrating against Moshe and Aharon. The people quarreled with Moshe. "We wish that we had died together with our brothers before God!" they declared. "Why did you bring God's congregation to this desert? So that we and our livestock should die? Why did you take us out of Egypt and bring us to this terrible place?

45. *Bemidbar* 14:2-3.
46. *Bemidbar* 16:13-14.
47. *Shemot* 17:2-7.

A Taste of Eden

It is an area where there are no plants, figs, grapes or pomegranates. [Now] there is not even any water to drink!" (20:2-5).

When we look at their words carefully and compare them to the earlier water crisis, a few significant but subtle differences come to our attention. In both cases, the perfunctory "Why did you take us out of Egypt and bring us to this terrible place?" is there, but other elements of their complaints are radically different: Now, the frame of reference has shifted. Rather than longing for the zucchini and watermelons of Egypt,[48] the people bemoan the lack of "figs, grapes and pomegranates"—the fruits of the Land of Israel. In other words, rather than demanding to return to Egypt, as they had in the past, they are complaining that they are not in the Land of Israel. Moreover, their complaint reveals a deep-seated God-consciousness: "'We wish that we had died together with our brothers before *God!*'" and, "'Why did you bring *God's* congregation to this desert?"

This is a new generation, and they have made great forward strides. Whereas their fathers lamented ever having left the security and familiarity of Egypt, the generation of the children laments the fact that they have not yet arrived in the Promised Land. Whereas the previous generation had the audacity to question whether or not God was in their midst, this new generation is acutely aware of God's presence, and of their own unique status as a covenantal community. This is not the same complaint that we have heard time and time again—yet Moshe fails to hear the difference between what they are saying and what their parents said. He fails to appreciate the nuances, and

---

48. *Bemidbar* 11:5.

Parashat Chukat

responds as if they are murmuring the same complaints. He accuses them of being "rebels" without pausing to consider the validity of this accusation: To be sure, they were unhappy with their lot, dissatisfied with life in the desert—but is this not as it should be? Should not every Jew who finds himself outside of the Land of Israel feel unsettled, dissatisfied, incomplete?

When we read their complaints carefully, a new picture emerges: These people were not looking back with fond nostalgia, they were pining for the future. Far from attempting to shirk the destiny that awaited them, they were over-eager to embrace it. Rather than complaining about the demands that their peoplehood placed upon them, they sought out God's presence. If they were to die, they preferred to die "in front of God." These people thirsted for holiness—the holiness of the Land of Israel, and of proximity to God.

Moshe suffered from pre-conceived notions of what the people wanted. Rather than listening to what they actually said, he heard echoes of the past. It was Moshe who was looking backward, mistakenly attributing the mindset of the previous generation to the people who now stood before him. Moshe's sin was one of missed opportunity. By responding to what he thought they had said, and not to what they actually said, he failed to sanctify God in the eyes of this new generation.

Part of belief in God is belief in the Jewish People; Moshe expresses a lack of faith in the new generation when he calls them rebels, and is therefore guilty of a lack of faith in God Himself. God reprimands him: The Jewish People—this new generation that stands before Moshe and demands holiness, the generation that expresses deep yearning for the Land of Israel and awareness of God's involvement in their lives—has faith. It is Moshe, and not the young nation, who has failed to move ahead. Moshe hears the complaints of the past; in a very real sense, both he and Aharon are a part of the previous generation—the generation that would not merit the Land of Israel. Therefore, Moshe and Aharon were sentenced to stay behind with their own generation, while this new generation would make their way to the Land for which they longed, the land of their dreams.

Parashat Balak
The Road Not Taken

The events recounted in *Parashat Balak* took place millennia ago, but so many of the elements of the story are all too familiar to the modern reader.

Although the actual conquest of the Land of Israel had not yet begun, there had already been a few military skirmishes between the Israelites and the tribes of Canaan and its environs. Generally, the conflicts centered around free passage through secure travel routes and use of water. Apparently things have not changed much in this part of the world.

The locals, an ad hoc coalition of erstwhile enemies, band together to wage war against the Jewish People, despite their age-old internecine warring. Motivated by fear of their common enemy, they resolve to mend their fractious ways in order to bar the Israelites' return to their ancestral homeland—again, a scenario that continues to repeat itself to this very day.

As opposed to the earlier conflicts recorded in the Torah, which were limited battles over access to resources or roads, the conflict in *Parashat Balak* introduces elements of religion and plain, old-fashioned anti-Semitism (even though this term would be coined only thousands of years later, and

169

the perpetrators in this particular episode were themselves Semites). The spokesperson for this coalition of tribes describes the People of Israel as a beast that destroys everything in its way, dehumanizing the Jews while giving voice to fear and dread in a propaganda effort that has been imitated over and over again, from the middle ages through Nazi Germany. Interestingly, this characterization stands in stark contrast to the self-perception voiced by the spies only a few chapters earlier in the text, who reported that when they compared themselves to the inhabitants of the Land, they were like grasshoppers in their own eyes, and assumed that the locals saw them the same way.

Rather than employing the military tactics that these states surely had at their disposal, they choose to hire a soothsayer to curse the Jews. Apparently they know, or at least sense, that the Jewish people are blessed who, barring some sort of major realignment, will soon return to their homeland. Their strategy is to strip the children of Avraham of their Divine protection.

As the story unfolds, this Divine protection is tested—and proven effective: Bil'am's calling card, the specialty he advertises, is a "skill set" purloined from the promise God made to Avraham: Whomever he blesses will be blessed and whomever he curses will be cursed. In the end, God protects the Jews from the curses of the smooth-tongued, misanthropic seer Bil'am, who is humiliated when it becomes clear that not only is he incapable of effectively cursing the Jews but his own donkey sees more than he does, and is apparently more eloquent as well.

When the coalition that hired Bil'am finally accepts the failure of their plan, they launch "Plan B," which proves far more effective: The Jews forfeit their Divine protection, not because of the hate-filled words hissed by some sorcerer, but because of their own debased behavior. The Midianite and Moavite women, who are sent to seduce the Jewish men and entangle them in pagan worship, prove to be a far more formidable enemy than the self-important, self-aggrandizing Bil'am.

Unfortunately, these nations never considered the third option, "Plan C," as it were: Why not try peace? Why not reach out and offer co-existence? Balak and the tribes he represented were well-aware that the Israelites were a blessed nation, that they were protected by a Divine covenant, that they would soon be returning to their ancestral homeland, that God Himself desired this particular course of events. Why not join forces with the Jews? Why not enter an alliance with them, and benefit from the blessings that would surely result from a partnership with God's chosen people? The power of the Jewish People was clear to them, as was the unique holiness of the Israelite way of life—but they were unwilling to embrace or even respect the holiness or defer to the power this holiness conferred upon the Jews. They chose, instead, to fight it. They were repulsed by the holiness, and the only plan they could conjure up was a plan of attack—either against the power of the Jewish People or against the holiness that gave them that power—but not a plan of peace. Once again, history lives.

Parashat Pinchas
Moshe's Mantle

As the Israelites move closer to the Land of Israel, issues of inheritance come to the fore. This is true regarding the Land itself, on the one hand, but also in terms of leadership on the other hand. Moshe, who will not enter the Land of Israel, raises the question: Who will be the new leader? Moshe insists that the People of God not be left leaderless: "Let God's community not be like sheep that have no shepherd'" (*Bemidbar* 27:17).

From the manner in which the request is made,[49] and from God's response, it seems that this is not simply a political or military appointment. The person God chooses will have the unenviable task of filling Moshe's shoes.

Replacing a legend in any industry is difficult; replacing Moshe seems impossible. In fact, a similar challenge is recorded in the Book of Kings, as the great prophet Eliyahu (Elijah) prepares to leave his student and heir Elisha. The master leaves his anxious student one final blessing or wish:

And it came to pass, when they had crossed over (the Jordan), Eliyahu said to Elisha, "Ask

---

49. In this section Moshe addresses God in an unusual manner: "Let the Omnipotent God of all living souls appoint a man over the community."

what I shall do for you, before I am taken away from you." And Elisha said, "I beg you, let a double portion of your spirit be upon me" (2 Kings 2:9).

In what might at first seem to be a haughty or presumptuous request, Elisha asks not for the power of his master, but for double the power, twice the capabilities of the great Eliyahu. In fact, Elisha was far from haughty or power-hungry. He was fully aware of the greatness of his teacher, of Eliyahu's unsurpassed gifts as a prophet and leader. If anything, Elisha felt inadequate to step into the enormous void that Eliyahu would leave behind, which led him to seek out some way to compensate for the shortfall in leadership and vision he foresaw. In Elisha's mind, only an endowment of twice the power, twice the insight and vision, would be enough to compensate for his own lack of talent. Only in this way would he, who paled in comparison to his great teacher, be able to meet the challenge and fulfill the needs of the soon-to-be-bereft generation.

In contrast, when He answers Moshe's plea for a replacement, God instructs him to take "take Yehoshua son of Nun, a man of spirit… and invest him with some of your splendor so that the entire Israelite community will obey him" (*Bemidbar* 27:18, 20).

Why should Elisha, the man chosen to replace Eliyahu, receive "twice the power" of his predecessor, while Yehoshua, the man chosen to replace Moshe, receive only "some of the splendor" of Moshe? To be sure, Moshe's prophetic ability was unique. No other human being before or since will ever achieve that proximity to God.[50] Therefore, by definition, Yehoshua

---

50. *Devarim* 34:10.

could not have been given "twice the power" of his teacher. But this does not explain why his mandate was so curiously limited from the outset.

We may say that this conundrum goes beyond the question of succession, and sheds light on the underlying issue that created the need for a change in leadership in the first place: Moshe could not enter the Land of Israel because, simply put, he was too great. The people could not completely understand or properly estimate Moshe's capabilities. Instead, his unique relationship with God became a crutch that they had come to rely upon too heavily. Had Moshe continued to lead them into the Land of Israel, they would have remained passive, simply standing by and waiting for miracles to solve their problems and fulfill their needs. They would have become spectators rather than participants in Jewish history.

When God gives *His* commentary on Moshe's death, He explains that Moshe was "guilty" of using too much of the power God had bestowed upon him.[51] By striking the rock, Moshe and Aharon gave the impression that they, and not God, were the source of this miracle. At this point in their development, the people had to be weaned from their reliance on miracles, from their expectation that miraculous events were the norm. The supernatural seemed natural to them. Now, their impending entrance into the Land of Israel would require them to shift into a different mode of existence: The manna would soon be replaced by agriculture, and their sustenance would no longer be insured through the agency of Moshe, Aharon, and Miriam. Rather than waiting for their leaders to perform miracles, the people would now become partners with God.

---

51. See *Devarim* 32:51 where the word *ma'altem*, "trespass," is used.

Parashat Pinchas

Eliyahu and Elisha lived in a time of religious anarchy. The people were deeply involved in idolatrous worship, and the novice Elisha would have to seamlessly take up the mantle of leadership once worn by Eliyahu. Elisha was well aware of what lay ahead, and he wisely asked to be endowed with even more power than his teacher: The Jewish People needed to see the power of God; anything less would have fallen short of what would be necessary to stem the tide of paganism that had washed over the nation. On the other hand, Moshe's generation had witnessed unparalleled miracles each and every day. They had no need for one more miracle. What they needed was to begin a new chapter, in which their own relationship with God would blossom and grow through the continuous acts of faith and adherence that would make up their everyday life in the Land of Israel. Moshe's unique, miraculous form of leadership was what they had needed in the wilderness; the next chapter would be written in a different style, under the leadership of a man who was endowed with a small portion of Moshe's spiritual capabilities—but with the capabilities most suited to the life that lay ahead of them in the Promised Land.

Parshiyot Mattot–Mas'ei
A Lush Land

After countless delays, punishments and disappointments, as the Jews draw tantalizingly close to the Promised Land, a strange request is made by the tribes of Reuven and Gad:

> They said, "If you would grant us a favor, let this land be given to us as our permanent property, and do not bring us across the Jordan" (*Bemidbar* 32:5).

These words must have been particularly painful to Moshe: He pined and prayed for permission to cross into the Land of Israel, while these tribes, Reuven and Gad, seek permission to do just the opposite. They hope to remain outside the Land, on the eastern bank of the Jordan River.

Moshe's initial response is far from enthusiastic, but subsequently terms and conditions are worked out to satisfy both sides: These tribes will take an active role in the conquest of the Promised Land, and only then will they return to the lush grazing land they have chosen outside of Israel proper.

The descendants of Gad and Reuven responded, "We will do whatever God has told us. We will cross over as a special force to the land of Canaan, and we shall then have our permanent hereditary property on [this] side of the Jordan" (*Bemidbar* 32:31-32).

Quietly, almost imperceptibly, when the deal is finalized, a third tribe materializes, and joins the other two tribes in Transjordan:

> To the descendants of Gad and Reuven, and to half the tribe of Menasheh (son of Yosef), Moshe then gave the kingdom of Sichon (king of the Amorites) and the kingdom of Og (king of the Bashan). [He gave them] the land along with the cities along its surrounding borders (*Bemidbar* 32:33).

For some unexplained reason, a third tribe, Menasheh is included in this arrangement. The Torah offers no explanation; various commentaries have attempted to fill in the gaps. Ramban suggests that the tribes of Reuven and Gad initiated the broadening of their "coalition" in an attempt to ameliorate their feelings of isolation. A considerable number of the members of Menasheh were persuaded that the "real (in the most concrete sense of the word) estate" already conquered by the Israelites on the eastern bank of the Jordan was preferable to the "theoretical" land that awaited them, as yet unconquered, on the other side. In Ramban's view, Menasheh joined the other two tribes in an arrangement motivated by greed; their only thought was of turning a "quick buck."

An almost diametrically opposed explanation is offered by the famed Rosh Yeshiva of Volozhin, Rabbi Naftali Tzvi Yehudah Berlin. In his view, the addition of the Menashites to this group was not initiated by any of the three tribes involved; rather, the "culprit" was Moshe himself. Moshe was the greatest leader of the Jewish People and as such, he was unwilling to leave part of his flock—especially those who seemed to be "ideologically challenged," who preferred the anticipated profits from their flocks to life in the Holy Land—all alone outside the borders of Israel. Moshe chose a group of people whom he felt he could trust to be the spiritual leaders and teachers of this far-flung community. Moshe hoped that these descendants of Yosef would follow their forefather's example, and take care of their brothers. He had faith in the power of Jewish community, and relied upon the mutual responsibility that members of all Jewish communities have to look after one another—socially and spiritually.

Was it greed or ideology, then, that led half the families of the tribe of Menasheh to join those who chose the verdant lands outside of Israel? In either case, their social experiment was neither successful nor long-lived. When the Children of Israel were cast into exile, these two-and-a-half tribes were the first to be carried off into captivity, the first to be lost. The East Bank never became a place that could boast about its thriving, vibrant, Torah-centric community. In fact, the only thing they might have boasted about was their identification with the mysterious, unmarked grave of a great Jew who very much wished to cross the Jordan—the man who was outraged by their request to stay outside the Land: Tragically, Moshe, our greatest teacher and our most faithful shepherd, was forced to remain just beyond the border, together with a few tribes who were, just as tragically, indifferent.

Parashat Devarim – Tisha B'Av
It's About Time

This *parashah* is the first in a new book, but for the most part it is a book that tells an old story, a book whose very existence is born of tragedy. Moshe is close to death; he will not cross over the Jordan River to the Land of Israel, and he opens his final series of speeches with a retrospective. How did we get here? Where did we go wrong? Can we avoid such mistakes in the future?

> These are the words that Moshe spoke to all Israel on the east bank of the Jordan.... An eleven day journey from Horev to Kadesh Barnea by way of the Se'ir highlands (*Devarim* 1:1-2).

The Jews have arrived at the cusp of the Holy Land, at the banks of a river that the disciples will cross without their master. After forty years of wandering, Moshe reveals that the actual distance between the Land of Israel and Horev (also known as Sinai), the place the detour began, is a mere eleven-day journey. So many years wasted, so many lives lost, and it all could have been avoided.

A Taste of Eden

How, indeed, had it come to this? At Horev, Moshe was first called upon to lead the Jewish People out of slavery. There, he saw a bush that burned but was not consumed, a symbol of eternity, of God's existence beyond the confines of space and time. This personal revelation was later shared with the entire Jewish People at that very same spot, just as God had promised Moshe at the start (*Shemot* 3:12): The personal, micro-revelation was transformed into a macro-revelation, the Revelation, that would forge a nation and change the world.

At that same spot, Moshe climbed to the summit and received a physical manifestation of the Revelation, the Tablets of Stone—and, at that very same spot, things went awry. The people panicked; it seemed to them that too much time had passed, and Moshe had not survived his encounter with God. Rather than putting their faith in Moshe's unique capabilities or in God's express commitment, they allowed fear to overtake them; they sought out an alternative to Moshe—and the golden calf was formed. How quickly they regressed! They had heard God Himself speak to them only 40 days earlier, but they managed to forget both the experience of that Revelation and its content. The roar of the frenzied crowd, the beating drums and rhythmic chants of the idolatrous orgy, drowned out the memory of the sights and sounds of the Revelation at Sinai.

Moshe's descent from the mountain, with the Tablets in his arms, should have been cause for celebration; that day should have been known for all time as "Simchat Torah," a day of rejoicing with the Torah. Instead, Moshe's return to the camp went unnoticed by the people below, who were too busy worshipping the golden calf to pay any attention to him or to the gift he had brought down to them. And then, at that very same spot, Moshe, who had no part in the inconceivable sin, prayed and pleaded for forgiveness on behalf of the nation. At that very spot, the detour began, and it is the narrative of that detour that comprises the last two books of the Torah— a long, arduous, 39-year trek that should have taken only eleven days.

When we stood at Sinai, we had been heartbreakingly close to our destination, but we lost track of time. We concerned ourselves with Moshe's tardiness, and paid no attention to the fact that we had, in fact, lost our grasp on time itself, and turned an eleven-day journey into decades of wandering.

Rashi offers a fascinating insight into this eleven-day distance: When we finally made the journey in earnest, it only took three days (see Rashi on *Devarim* 1:2).

In fact, this peculiar, kaleidoscopic time-line is more relevant to our lives than it might seem at first glance. Time is a strange and slippery concept: Often, there are life-lessons that normally take years to learn, which can be acquired in a flash, in a lightning-bolt of clarity, in what is known as an "aha moment." On the long and winding road, a short and direct route is suddenly illuminated. Other times, we see the light yet repeatedly ignore the message; repeating the same mistakes over and over, we force ourselves to take unnecessary detours and to expend our emotional, intellectual and physical energy going around in circles.

Our normal perception of time is linear and constant, but we are, by and large, "captives on a carousel of time," unable to break through, to transcend. Yet there are some people (and some situations) who manage to break these boundaries. Unfortunately, it often takes a cataclysm to grab our attention. We are only shaken out of our reverie by personal or national

A Taste of Eden

crises—or worse. This is the lesson of the first few words of the Book of *Devarim*: It took the Jewish People thirty-nine years to achieve what we should have accomplished in eleven days, but when we were finally ready—spiritually alert, attentive, and willing to step up and meet our destiny—the eleven-day journey was completed in three days.

All these years after the destruction of the Temple, it is clear to us that we have taken a two-thousand-year detour. But it should be equally clear to us that we are—and always have been—heartbreakingly close to our destination. The final distance can be achieved in days, minutes, perhaps even seconds—when we are finally ready to take those last few steps toward holiness.

Parashat Va'etchanan
The Crucible

The great tragedy of Moshe's life was the fact that he did not complete his mission; he would not bring the people to the Promised Land. In fact, we might say that this is actually two tragedies: On a personal level, it is almost inconceivable that Moshe, our greatest leader and teacher, our staunchest defender and most dedicated shepherd, would not see the Land of Israel up close, not be forgiven and allowed to reap the rewards of his years of unflinching dedication. On the other hand, Moshe's fate symbolizes a national tragedy: The entire generation that had experienced the wonders of the Exodus, the splitting of the sea, the Revelation at Mount Sinai and so much more, would also perish in the desert. The land would be inherited and enjoyed by their children.

Moshe begs to see the land. God understands precisely what it is that Moshe prays for, and although He commands Moshe to desist from further entreaties, God does, in fact, fulfill Moshe's prayer in a very literal sense. Moshe is allowed to climb to a mountaintop vantage point and "see the land," but only from afar.

A Taste of Eden

As Moshe continues his speech to the young generation who will soon go where he is not permitted to tread, it becomes painfully obvious to them that Moshe will not be joining them for the final leg of the journey. He takes this last opportunity to warn them about the consequences of idolatry, and pleads with them to keep the commandments in order to insure that the inheritance they are about to receive not be forfeited.

We may wonder how Moshe's final words were received by this young, eager generation. Did they find it incongruous that Moshe, the greatest man they had ever known, the man who now stands before them and exhorts them about right and wrong, sin and its punishment, will himself be banned from entering the Land? Were they perhaps intimidated by the knowledge that even Moshe, who was the greatest prophet who ever lived, was unable to live up to God's standards? Were they disheartened by the thought that if Moshe had fallen short, it seemed impossible that any mortal could succeed?

Apparently, Moshe was sensitive to these unspoken doubts and ruminations. As he begins his final series of lectures, he describes his personal predicament in very particular language, using an unusual turn of phrase that may give us a glimpse of his frame of mind and allow us to share his perspective. While other nations may worship the sun and moon and stars, he explains, the Jewish People is different. "But you, God Himself took, and He brought you out of the iron crucible that was Egypt, so that you would be His heritage nation, as you are today" (*Devarim* 4:20). While the image of the fiery crucible has captured the imagination of many commentaries and remains an enduring metaphor for Jewish history, Moshe may have had a very particular idea in mind when he first coined the phrase.

Parashat Va'etchanan

Rashi's comments on this verse are terse; he explains that the crucible reference means that the Jews are like gold, but does not elaborate. Two nineteenth-century scholars explained this passage at length, coming to widely divergent conclusions: Rabbi Yaakov Zvi Mecklenburg (1785-1865) refers to the process of smelting in which metals are purified of dross, and explains that the period of enslavement in Egypt had the same purpose: The Jews were subjected to a painful process that rid them of those who were unworthy, in order to allow them to meet their destiny unencumbered by those who would hold them back. This human dross would have fomented even more unrest and rebellion, and would have been unwilling and unable to receive the Torah or to fulfill the covenant they would undertake as a nation.

Rabbi Shimshon Raphael Hirsch (1808-1888) had a very different approach. Rather than intimating that there were impurities in the Jewish nation that had to be "burned off" in the fiery furnace of Egyptian slavery, Rabbi Hirsch saw the crucible as an experience that gave strength and polish to the morals of the newly-emerging nation. The fires destroyed everything that had been before, allowed the Jews to distill their essential qualities and hone their identity. It is this view of the crucible that may allow us to understand Moshe's words: His reference to the crucible is his attempt to point out one of the defining characteristics of Jewish nationhood. We are a people with a great capacity to suffer because we have a profound ability to see the long-term repercussions of our actions. Our enslavement in Egypt had not come as a surprise; not only was it foretold to Avraham, it was willingly accepted by him and his descendants as part of a long-term covenant. Avraham's children would inherit the Land of Israel, they would become a covenantal community and enjoy a unique relationship with God—but only after 400 years of exile, hardship and slavery. Yaakov accepted this birthright with all its conditions; he and his children, the very core of the Jewish People, were willing to suffer in the "short term" in order to achieve the long-term "payoff." Only a people with complete faith in the future, only those who are willing to postpone gratification in favor of a much greater spiritual destiny, are capable of accepting a covenant of this kind.

Long before Nietzsche's *Twilight of the Idols*, Moshe reminded us that the crucible of Egypt and the experience of slavery did not break us, did not eradicate us as a family or as a covenantal community, did not corrupt our morals; it not only made us stronger, it made us who we are. As he stands at the borders of the Promised Land but is denied entrance, Moshe himself is a living example that gratification of personal desires is far less important to the Jewish ethos than is the larger national destiny. Moshe is able to accept a world in which he is denied his heart's desire, he is able to withstand his personal pain and frustration, because he has complete faith in the future of the Jewish People and the Word of God.

Moshe's message to the nation moves seamlessly from an account of his own personal pain to an inspiring account of the strength of his beloved people, even in the face of setbacks that lasted many generations. They have come through the crucible as a nation and they are gold, they are strong, they have been endowed with greatness. The suffering and humiliation, even the death of loved ones that they experienced in the crucible of slavery, has made them stronger, more united, more determined,

Parashat Va'etchanan

as well as more aware of the suffering of others. They have refined the ability they inherited from their forefathers to take the long view, to see past the setbacks, even when these have been tragic and extreme. And now, they must see past the death of their greatest prophet and leader. Jewish history, Moshe reminds them, is measured in millennia, not in minutes, and he assures them that they have what it takes to begin the next chapter—just as we, even today, so many generations and so many setbacks later, have what it takes to march toward the fulfillment of our glorious destiny.

Parashat Ekev
Rain

This past week was a difficult one here in Israel. There were two separate incidents of murder and attempted murder: First, a man who, based on his external dress, could be called an orthodox, or even ultra-orthodox Jew, attacked other Jews in the center of Jerusalem. Second, an Arab family was attacked, resulting in the death of their youngest child, a toddler named Ali; although the investigation is still underway, the evidence appears to indicate that the perpetrator or perpetrators are, again, "observant" Jews. In both cases, the victims of this unthinkable violence were the very members of society who often feel most persecuted and vulnerable: the gay community on the one hand, and the Arab community on the other.

For two thousand years, Jews have endured one particular challenge in almost every corner of the globe: They have lived as a persecuted minority. With the establishment of the State of Israel, a new challenge emerged: Suddenly, for the first time in millennia, we have been forced to grapple with the challenge of being in charge, of being the majority. So many long-forgotten issues arose with the re-establishment of Jewish sovereignty: How will minority groups be treated in the Jewish State? How will those who are "different" be made to feel? Will we protect those "others"—the disenfranchised, the outsiders—or will we make them feel vulnerable?

Although *Parashat Ekev* does not address this topic directly, we may gain insight into the Jewish approach to communal life through Moshe's final lessons to the Jews as they prepare to enter the Land. Moshe speaks about the need to obey the word of God, to obey the commandments. The consequence of disobedience, he warns them, is drought (*Devarim* 11:16-17). Conversely, if the people follow the will of God, we are assured that rain will fall in the proper quantity and season; economic success is insured (*Devarim* 11:13-15).

What is clear from this section is that the resulting prosperity is collective, and not individual. The rain will not fall only on my crops while my neighbor's field suffers from drought. The experience of living in a country—especially our country, the Land of Israel, which has a particularly sensitive spiritual constitution—is one of collective economic destiny. Famine, as well as plenty, is a shared reality, and is the result of the behavior of the collective.

There are those who would argue that precisely because of this shared destiny, the religiously sensitive person must step up, take the law into his or her own hands, and insure that the Torah's commandments are obeyed and enforced. This approach leads to vigilantism of the type we have been subjected to this past week, and it is anathema to Judaism.

From the dawn of our history, Judaism has abhorred murder. The seven Noachide laws (*Bereishit* 9:5-6) applied to Jews before the covenant at Sinai, and the Ten Commandments include the prohibition of murder (*Shemot* 20:13). Rambam describes why the taking of a life is considered so severe:

> Although there are other sins that are more serious than murder, they do not present as serious a danger to society as murder does. Even idol worship—and needless to say, sexual sins or the violation of the Sabbath—are not considered as severe as murder, for these other sins involve man's relationship with God, while murder also involves man's relationship with his fellow man.

> Whoever commits this sin is an utterly wicked person. All the *mitzvot* that he performs throughout his lifetime cannot outweigh this sin or save him from judgment. ("Laws of Murder and Preservation of Life" 4:9)

The sin of murder eclipses any good deeds the murderer has done or will do in the future. Thus, a person dressed in "religious garb" who commits murder—is simply a murderer in religious garb, no more and no less. Neither the choice of clothing nor any other religious behavior or affectation will save him or her when the time comes to stand before God and be judged. A murderer may clothe himself in any fashion he chooses, but he is naked in terms of spirituality.

According to Rambam, murder is the most terrible sin precisely because it poses the gravest threat to human society. Taking another person's life (other than in cases of self-defense)—no matter who they are or what you believe them to be guilty of—causes the delicate fabric of society to unravel.[52] Murder pollutes the collective, undermines society at its most basic level—and makes prosperity impossible for each and every individual as well as for society as a whole.

---

52. Rabbi Meir Simcha of Dvinsk (1843-1926), in his commentary to the Torah, *Meshech Chochmah* (*Shemot* 21:14), opines that the killing of a non-Jew is even worse than the killing of a Jew.

Parashat Re'eh
Non-Prophets

It seems as if the dearth of leadership is, and always has been, a perpetual problem. We have a tendency to search for people who can inspire and lead us; unfortunately, the role models we choose are rarely vetted in any systematic or rigorous way, and we tend to choose charisma over substance. Since the very dawn of human history, as far back as the Garden of Eden, we have been seduced by charismatic hucksters who offer slick sound-bytes that obfuscate truth and lead us astray.

Spiritual leaders are even harder to evaluate. By definition, the spiritual leader has knowledge, skills, and a particular type of power that his or her followers lack. The gap that divides the leader and the neophyte often makes the leader appear inscrutable, beyond our limited ability to judge or evaluate.

In *Parashat Re'eh*, as Moshe's reign winds down, attention is turned to establishing the next generation of leadership. Various positions must be filled, leadership roles must be defined and appointments made. In subsequent chapters, the Torah will outline the respective mandates of kings, judges and other public servants, but first and foremost, Moshe lays out the parameters for a very peculiar sort of religious leader:

the prophet, and not just any prophet, but a man or woman who produces "signs and wonders." This person is capable of bending the laws of nature, of suspending the physical rules of the universe, and foretelling the future with stunning accuracy. What, we may ask, could possibly be better than having a *bona fide* prophet as a spiritual leader?

Remarkably, the Torah warns us to reserve judgment. Miraculous abilities are not necessarily a sign of authenticity; knowledge of the future is not an indication that this person should be followed blindly. Unlike so much of modern communication, the medium is not necessarily the message; the question should always be one of substance over form. What is this person advising, commanding or instructing us to do? Are the "prophet's" words consonant with the words of Moshe, or does this person simply possess strange, unexplained talents and charisma?

If, for example, the prophet—after performing wondrous acts—advocates worship of an alien deity, we are commanded to reject their leadership. Despite his or her unique, unexplainable abilities, this "prophet" is regarded as the most dangerous of all leaders. If the message is corrupt, self-serving, exploitive, this person is not one whom God or Moshe would encourage us to follow.

Throughout history, we have failed in this area time and time again. Sincere people have been, and continue to be, deceived by charlatans. We have had our share of impressive false prophets and messiahs, yet we do not seem to learn. Despite our sophistication and worldliness, despite the bitter experience we have accrued, we lack the discernment that should prevent us from falling prey to snake oil salesmen and bogus prophets. We

A Taste of Eden

still want shortcuts to spirituality, and would rather stand in line to receive the blessings and bogus insights of false spiritual gurus than take the time and make the effort to seek out truth. Charismatic individuals will always be able to satisfy their own base desires for adulation and obedience at the expense of those who choose form over substance in their quest for a quick spiritual fix.

Moshe's warning is clear, and it is as relevant today as ever: It all comes down to substance. When a charismatic leader arises, if he (or she) does not unequivocally advocate adherence to the Torah, that person must be regarded as a false prophet.

Apparently, the essential role of the prophet was to serve as the leader against idolatry, the spiritual counter to idolatry. Even true prophets, who stood strong against false and counterfeit spirituality, stood the risk of being sucked into the world of the occult, of becoming part of the problem rather than the solution. When the desire to worship idols was banished, prophecy, too, became a thing of the past; it was no longer needed, no longer possible. When there was no longer a rapacious hunger for idolatry, had prophecy been allowed to continue without its counter-balance, it would have upset the delicate balance and destroyed the spiritual ecosystem.

Today, we have neither the overpowering urge to worship other gods nor access to prophecy. And yet, even in today's world, rife as it is with scandals involving religious and secular leaders, a system of spiritual checks and balances is just as important. Recent events are no different than they have ever been in this sphere, and it behooves us to take a moment to question our own judgment, to oversee our "leaders," and to educate ourselves and those around us. We must not to be

194

impressed by "signs and wonders," by those with the gifts of charisma or clairvoyance. We must ask ourselves, "Is this leader the solution, or just another aspect of the problem?"

The genuine article, a real spiritual leader, brings us closer to God. That is ultimately the litmus test; anything else is fraudulent. If a prophet is "for profit," he or she is no prophet. If a spiritual leader is exploitive—financially, emotionally or sexually—he or she is not the leader we are looking for. If, on the other hand, he or she educates, inspires, and brings us closer to God, we have found someone to learn from and be inspired by. We have found a true leader.

Parashat Shoftim
Democracy, Theocracy, and Monarchy

Running any enterprise, whether it is a home, a business, or a country, is complex. As in so many other aspects of life, a delicate balance must be struck between competing considerations.

In *Parashat Shoftim*, the Israelites' time in the desert nears its end, and a new reality awaits them on the other side of the Jordan River. As they begin the next phase of their life as a nation in their homeland, Israel will face the dilemma of competing considerations, and much of *Parashat Shoftim* is taken up with issues that must be resolved in order for the new commonwealth to thrive.

In the desert, Moshe is the supreme leader. In a certain sense, he has the authority and status of king, despite what seems an almost conscious avoidance of the trappings of monarchy on his part. He is also the supreme religious leader. As it is clear that Moshe will not be crossing the Jordan with them, a new tension arises: How will their new country be governed? What is to be the form of authority? Will their nation-state be a monarchy or a theocracy? Which of the roles filled by Moshe will take precedence, and how will the polity be structured?

Parashat Shoftim

The concept of kingship is introduced in this *parashah*, but, surprisingly, not as a command but as a possibility. It appears that the king described in the Torah is appointed, if not elected, by the people: Should they choose to appoint a monarch, he is to be invested with substantial, but not absolute, authority and power.

On the other hand, this same *parashah* introduces the court system, which has both judicial and legislative powers. This system of courts is deemed the final arbiter in all instances of interpersonal conflict or religious issues. Whenever a clarification of law or a decision regarding its application is required, we are instructed to turn to the courts, and not to the king, for a decision (*Devarim* 17:8-13). The court of which the Torah speaks is what we might call a "religious court," and it stands as a counter-balance to the monarchy.

The era of the "one man show," in which Moshe stood at the top of both the political and the judicial/religious systems, would now come to an end. Instead, two competing arms of government would be established: a democratically appointed monarch, and a legal system based on the principle of majority.

Let us consider this first institution, the seemingly oxymoronic "democratically selected monarch." A careful reading of Maimonides' "Law of Kings" is instructive:

Once a king is anointed, he and his descendants are granted the monarchy for eternity, for the monarchy is passed down by inheritance, as it states: "Thus, the king and his descendants will prolong their reign in the midst of Israel" (*Devarim* 17:20).... This applies if the knowledge and the fear of God of the son is equivalent to that of his ancestors. If his fear of God is equivalent to theirs but not his knowledge, he should be granted his father's position and given instruction. However, under no circumstance should a person who lacks fear of God be appointed to any position in Israel, even though he possesses much knowledge. ("Laws of Kings" 1:7)

Surprising as this may seem, despite the creation of a monarchy which is passed down from generation to generation through a chosen family line, the chain of inheritance is not guaranteed. A determination must be made that the heir to the throne is in fact a worthy successor. The question is, who decides? Who determines whether the king is fit, and whether or not his descendants are worthy? Apparently, this power is in the hands of the people (perhaps through the agency of their representatives on the Great Court, the *Sanhedrin HaGadol*). The process through which this power is exercised creates the contours of a unique type of democracy.

The power of the monarch is subject to even more stringent limits from another quarter: Aside from the role of the people in choosing to appoint a king and approving the chain of inheritance of the monarchy, the king is subject to the laws of the Torah as they are interpreted and applied by the Great Court. The judicial-legislative arm of government stands above the monarchy; the political arm of government is secondary to the theological arm of government. We may say, then, that the system of governance prescribed in *Parashat Shoftim* is a democratically conceived monarchy ruled by theocracy. Modern Western sensibilities might cringe at this sort of hybrid, and we might imagine the impossible tension that this system would create. However, the force intended to ameliorate this tension is part and parcel of the mandate of the king:

> When [the king] is established on his royal throne, he must write a copy of this Torah… [which] must always be with him, and he shall read from it all the days of his life. He will then learn to be in awe of God his Lord, and carefully keep every word of this Torah and these rules. (*Devarim* 17:18-19)

With one elegant stroke, the Torah establishes the dialectic, the mechanism that will maintain the delicate balance: The king, despite his power and authority, must remain in a constant state of attentiveness to the Torah and its laws. He must never forget the true nature of the mandate with which he has been entrusted, and must remain mindful of the true source of his authority—and its limits. Keeping the Torah close to his heart and mind at all times will help him stay in touch, stay grounded, and remain accountable to those below him, parallel with him, and, most particularly, to the One above.

The ideal Jewish polity described in this *parashah* is based on a system of checks and balances: a judicial system comprised of the wisest and most honest religious leaders, combined with a king selected by the people, all of whom are bound by the Torah, the immutable word of God. While this combination does not guarantee success, its very structure reminds us where our priorities should lie. In fact, we may say that the system of governance described in *Parashat Shoftim* is, in and of itself, a brief mission statement for the Jewish nation-state.

Parashat Ki Tetzei
Another Brick in the Wall

Over the past few chapters we have noted a gradual shift in the topics Moshe addresses as he imparts his final lessons to the Jewish People. From an extensive polemic against idolatry, the focus shifts to the building of the Temple, and then moves on to other national institutions such as the establishment and mandate of courts, the monarchy and prophets. To a large extent, this *parashah* narrows the lens, moving to commandments of a more interpersonal or individual nature. Though Moshe touches upon many commandments, one particular topic is mentioned numerous times: marriage.[53] Although much of the discussion revolves around what might be called "unconventional relationships"—the wife taken as a captive of war, polygamy and preference of one wife above the other, and more—there is one brief mention of love, marriage and happiness.

> When a man takes a new bride, he shall not enter military service or be assigned to any associated duty. He must remain free for his family for one year, and rejoice with his bride. (*Devarim* 24:5)

53. This essay is dedicated to the marriage of our son Yosef Dov to Shoval Cohen.

Parashat Ki Tetzei

The *Sefer HaChinuch*, an early (anonymous) book of *mitzvot*, notes that the concept of marriage is a stark, polar opposite to the sexual promiscuity that is mentioned earlier in this *parashah* (*Devarim* 23:18). The selection of one special person, as described poetically by Adam[54] in the Garden of Eden, is the ideal:

> A man shall therefore leave his father and mother and cling to his wife, and they shall become one flesh. (*Bereishit* 2:24)

One man, one woman; this a relationship of exclusivity.

In a sense, the nature of marriage mirrors the relationship outlined earlier in *Devarim* regarding the Beit HaMikdash. We are told to serve God in one chosen, special place:

> Do away with all the places where the nations whom you are driving out worship their gods, [whether they are] on the high mountains, on the hills, or under any luxuriant tree…. You may not worship the Almighty God in such a manner. This you may do only on the site that the Almighty God will choose from among all your tribes, as a place established in His name. It is there that you shall go to seek His presence. (*Devarim* 12:2-5)

While the idolaters worshiped under every tree and upon every hill and high place, the Jews were commanded to worship God exclusively in one centralized place—a place later identified

---

54. There are those who claim this declaration was an "editorial" statement made by God.

as the Temple Mount in Jerusalem. We might say that the difference between the Jewish approach to worship and the idolatrous approach is the difference between a "one-night stand" and a marriage, between promiscuity and the union of two people joined in holiness. Idolatry, particularly regarding the element of immediate gratification, is spiritual promiscuity.

When a bride and groom rejoice in one another, their happiness stems in no small part from the joy of exclusivity, from the knowledge that their chosen partner is the only person with whom they will share the holiness of marriage and sexual intimacy. This is happiness born of holiness. In this context, the Talmud teaches us that not only is it incumbent upon the husband to bring joy and happiness to his spouse, but all those who attend the wedding are commanded to bring happiness to the new couple. In fact, the Talmud (*Berachot* 6b) goes so far as to say that whoever successfully brings joy to the bride and groom, is considered to have rebuilt "one of the ruins of Jerusalem."

As we know, *the* ruin of Jerusalem is the Temple itself, a building dedicated to the exclusive relationship between God and His People. When the people "cheated" on God, as was the case during the First Temple era, or simply took their relationship with Him for granted, as was the case during the Second Temple era, the Temple was destroyed. On the personal scale, marriage, with its essential component of exclusivity, serves as a metaphor for the relationship between man and God; in essence, it is a microcosm of that relationship. When a husband and wife find joy in the holiness of marriage, they build not only their own interpersonal relationship, but also the community as a whole, as well as the relationship between man and God. They become partners in the rebuilding of the Temple.

Parashat Ki Tetzei

Every Jewish home is holy. In a sense, every Jewish home is a microcosm of the Holy Temple. Therefore, every happy Jewish home serves as a step to the complete rebuilding of Jerusalem.

Parashat Ki Tavo
Gratitude

The life that awaits the Children of Israel in the Promised Land will hold many challenges alongside its rewards, and in *Parashat Ki Tavo* Moshe turns the spotlight on both sides of this coin.

The Land of Israel is unlike any other place in the world. It is a land imbued with a spiritual personality, a delicate constitution that will not tolerate sin. On the other hand, avoiding sin is not enough. Living in Israel will entail additional obligations, and in this *parashah* Moshe describes one of these additional *mitzvot: bikkurim.*

The mitzvah of *bikkurim* will be fulfilled long after his own passing, after the conquest of the Land and the division of the tribal portions, after homes are built, after fields and orchards and vineyards are planted and the first harvest is gathered. This, Moshe explains, will not be ordinary produce; this is holy fruit of the Holy Land, and it will require special treatment: The very first fruit, the produce that has been so anxiously awaited, is to be placed in a basket and carried to Jerusalem. With this precious harvest in hand, the farmer is commanded to recite a specific text, recounting a brief history of the Jewish People. The ritual is designed to place the celebration of the harvest into

Parashat Ki Tavo

historical as well as spiritual context, culminating in the harvest that symbolizes our status as a free and holy nation.

As we read Moshe's description of *bikkurim*, the ritual of the First Fruits, we might take a moment to consider the contrast with the other "first fruits" mentioned in the Torah—the very first fruits, in the Garden of Eden. The reality in which Adam and Eve existed was unique: Their proximity to God Himself, the immediacy of their connection to His Presence, and the symbiosis of that spirituality with the well-being of the Garden and its holy fruits are echoed in the reality into which the Israelites would enter as they crossed the Jordan. However, the earlier experience, the experiment of entrusting man with the holy fruits in Eden, was a failure, ending in disaster and exile. Careful consideration of the *bikkurim* ceremony gives us the sense that the mitzvah we are commanded to perform with the first fruits is in some way a *"tikkun,"* a type of spiritual healing for the misappropriation of those very first fruits of the Garden: First and foremost, Adam and Eve had allowed themselves to be convinced by the Serpent that eating the forbidden fruit would somehow transform them into gods.[55] The *bikkurim* ritual is a direct and unmistakable counter to that sort of self-centered delusion. Jewish farmers take their most precious harvest in hand, and remind themselves how it came to be. Rather than self-congratulation for their resourcefulness and success, they consciously, even demonstrably, thank God for this produce.

In two separate comments, Rashi elucidates a second element of the sin in the Garden of Eden.

---

55. *Bereishit* 3:5.

A Taste of Eden

God called to the man, and He said, "Where are you [trying to hide]?" "I heard Your voice in the garden," [Adam] replied, "and I was afraid because I was naked, so I hid." [God] asked, "Who told you that you are naked? Did you eat from the tree which I commanded you not to eat?" The man replied, "The woman that you gave to be with me—she gave me what I ate from the tree." (*Bereishit* 3:9-12)

The very fact that God engaged man in conversation indicates that at this point all was not lost; there may yet have been words or gestures of repentance or conciliation to be said. But instead of expressing remorse, Adam points an accusative finger at his wife, the soul mate provided by God. Essentially, Adam blames everyone but himself for his moral lapse. Instead of saying "thank you" for being introduced to the woman of his dreams, Adam attempts to shift all the blame to her. Rashi[56] labels this behavior "a lack of gratitude," a lack of appreciation for what God has provided. In a very real sense, this lack of gratitude is "original sin." God created man with limitations and foibles; that was always a part of the design. We might say that the transgression of eating from the forbidden fruit was not nearly as disappointing as what ensued: The true test of man is not in whether or not he will fail; inevitably, almost unavoidably, he will. The greater test lies not only in taking responsibility for his actions—and his failures—but in his ability to recognize, appreciate and give thanks for the gifts that God bestows upon him.

Commenting on the mitzvah of *bikkurim* and on the verses that make up the text of its ritual, Rashi illustrates how the

---

56. Rashi, *Bereishit* 3:12.

historical and theological context it creates is designed to teach us to be grateful and at the same time allow us an opportunity to express that gratitude.[57]

Appreciation for what God does for us is the foundation of religious life. Appreciation for what other human beings do for us is the foundation of decency and, by extension, a decent society. The greatest enemy of this sort of decency is the overdeveloped sense of entitlement from which modern man too often suffers. It blinds us to the wonderful gifts God gives us, deludes us into thinking that this is God's responsibility, His "job description." Similarly, we are often guilty of belittling or taking for granted what other people do for us, even when, and especially when, it is in their "job description." We expect service because we "deserve" it, but are we appreciative when we get it? Do we express that appreciation? Do we allow the other person to feel our appreciation?

The experience in the Garden of Eden was a microcosm of life in the Land of Israel: Misbehavior results in expulsion, exile. The fruit of the Garden, like the fruit of the Land, belongs to God. We are given sustenance as a gift from His hand. The farmers who toil in the Land of Israel are allowed to partner with Him in this holy endeavor, but they must never forget the true source of our sustenance. The *bikkurim* ritual, and the joyous way in which it is performed, allow us to thank God—and all His messengers who live among us, whom He sends to protect and provide for us each and every day—for our bountiful, miraculous sustenance.

---

57. Rashi, *Devarim* 26:3.

Parashat Nitzavim
A Holy Collective

As Moshe prepares to leave the stage of Jewish history, he invokes a covenant between God and the Jewish People. This is neither the first nor the only time a covenant is discussed, but here in *Parashat Nitzavim* Moshe introduces an element never clearly stated before:

> I am not forging this covenant and this oath with you alone; I am creating this bond with those of you who are standing here with us today before God, as well as those who are not here with us today. (*Devarim* 29:13-14)

The covenant includes all those who were present at that time, but so much more: This is a trans-generational covenant. All future generations are bound by this agreement as if they themselves had stood on the eastern shore of the Jordan River and heard Moshe's parting speech, as if they had witnessed the forming of the covenantal community with their own eyes, as if they themselves had signed, as it were, on the dotted line. This is not a particularly strange feature of the agreement: Individuals often find themselves subject to agreements in which they were not active participants. Governments, corporations and individuals often make pacts that obligate others. Nonetheless, this particular agreement has profound ramifications, for it creates a new entity, a new concept: The Jewish People.

The Nation of Israel consists of the sum total of all Jews in the world, but not merely the sum total of all living Jews. The Jewish Nation is an aggregate that includes all Jews who have ever or will ever live. The covenant forged before Moshe's death specifically includes future generations as well, and, by extension, applies not only to the covenant itself, but to all of the intellectual, spiritual and physical assets that the covenant accrues. The Land of Israel, then, is given to the collective People of Israel, and not only to those who were present when it was promised to them or even those who actively participated in the conquest. Each generation is therefore considered caretakers, not owners; the Land of Israel is the property, the birthright, the inheritance of the entire trans-generational collective. Similarly, the Torah was entrusted to those who stood at Mount Sinai, but it "belongs" to all of Israel. It is the spiritual birthright of each and every member of the collective. A teacher who refuses to teach Torah to any Jewish student is, in fact, withholding the rightful inheritance of an heir, denying the rightful owner of this intellectual and spiritual treasure access to what is theirs. Every teacher is an executor of a spiritual estate, and each and every teacher must see to it that the heirs—who may not be aware of their rights or may be incapable of fully appreciating the value of their inheritance—receive and cherish what is legally theirs.

There is, however, another side to this covenantal relationship. Because each and every Jew is a part of this larger collective, mutual responsibility is its unavoidable result; this

A Taste of Eden

is one of the most well-known aspects of Judaism. However, we might not have been aware of the scope of this mutual responsibility: Just as the covenant spans all past and future generations, so, too, does our responsibility for one another. A Talmudic passage illustrates this point: Tractate *Rosh Hashanah* (32b) records a tradition that the angels complained to God that on Rosh Hashanah and Yom Kippur the Jews do not sing the hymns of praise that make up the Hallel Prayer. God Himself came to the Israelites' defense, explaining that these are days of judgment, during which "the books of the living and the books of the dead are opened" before Him, making this an inappropriate time for songs of thanksgiving, joy and praise. Interestingly, the text does not refer to the more familiar "Books of Life and Death," or the heavenly ledgers in which all human deeds are recorded and counted on these fateful days of judgment. Instead, the books of those "living and dead" are opened. Surely, the book of the living must be opened in order to judge each person according to their deeds and merits, but why, we might ask, is the book of those who have passed on from the mortal world opened as well? Surely they are beyond judgment! Not so, we are taught: During the Days of Awe, the dead—even those who died long ago—are judged, not for their actions during the passing year, but for the impact they have had on the world they left behind.

Here, then, is the trans-generational covenant of mutual responsibility in action: The actions of the present generation impact the judgment that is handed down regarding those who came before them. By their actions, the living have the power to give new meaning to the lives of members of the community

Parashat Nitzavim

who came before them, to transform and elevate their legacy in this world and their spiritual existence in the world beyond our own.

At this time of year, as we are ponder the power of *teshuvah* (repentance) to change the past, to turn our mistakes or transgressions into positive growth experiences, we should also consider the impact we might have on the more distant past. On a personal level, *teshuvah* is both liberating and redemptive. It allows us to make a clean break, to free ourselves from the stain that we have inflicted on our own souls. Mistakes can be corrected; lessons can be learned. We can change our own past, and be energized and elevated by our newfound relationship with God. At times, the sin that is truly and wholeheartedly repented can become the strongest part of a person's religious identify. This may be compared to a rope that is severed, and rejoined by a tight knot that becomes the strongest part of the entire rope. Moreover, the knotted rope, a metaphor for the relationship between man and God, is now shorter than before; the distance between man and God has become smaller. The sin and subsequent *teshuvah* bring man closer to God than he was before.

The lesson of *Parashat Nitzavim*, though, goes even further than this personal bond with God, for we now understand that the trans-generational nature of the covenant allows us to share in the redemption of past generations as well. By upholding the covenant, we build our own relationship with God, while at the same time we impact the generations that preceded us in the covenantal community. We can give meaning to the sacrifices made by our ancestors, or redeem the opportunities that our predecessors may have missed. We can be inspired by positive deeds of relatives who may otherwise have been forgotten, and bring the collective Jewish people closer to God and closer to realizing our glorious shared destiny. Such is the nature of this covenant; such is the nature of the Jewish People.

Parashat Vayelech
The End of the Shemittah Year:
An Opportunity to Begin Again

Every week, as Shabbat comes to a close, we mark the departure of the Shabbat Queen with a short *havdalah* ceremony, as one weekly cycle ends and the next begins.

Often, *havdalah* leaves a bittersweet taste in its wake. On the one hand, we are forced to lower the curtain on our much-needed day of rest, and return to the mundane concerns of our daily life.

On the other hand, the day's end also frees us from the many prohibitions of Shabbat.

Even one of the greatest Jewish philosophers of the modern era, Rabbi Joseph Soloveitchik, admitted that despite its holiness, the limitations to creativity and action that Shabbat observance places upon us can be "annoying."

In much the same way, as the end of the Jewish year approaches, we are on the cusp of a new annual cycle as well as a new seven-year *shemittah* cycle. As the sun sets on the last day of 5775 and we usher in the new year, we simultaneously take leave of the *shemittah* year, its unique holiness—and its unique restrictions. Although there is no *havdalah* ceremony to

A Taste of Eden

mark this transition, we would be well served by putting some thought into the start of a new seven-year cycle.

The desire to live in the Land of Israel is multifaceted. For some of us, it is mainly an outgrowth of our awareness and desire to connect to this land's history, while for others the excitement of building Israel's future is the strongest bond.

There are those for whom Israel is a natural expression of our peoplehood, while others are swept up by the holiness of this unique place—holiness which is often associated with the very earth beneath our feet, the ground on which our patriarchs and matriarchs carved out our national ethos, the fields and plains that have served as the bedrock of our national history for millennia.

Jewish law has always addressed this holiness, serving as a tool to heighten our awareness and connection to the land itself. The laws of the sabbatical year are a primary example, but they are much more: By encompassing aspects of spirituality, social justice and socioeconomics, they mirror many other facets of our national existence.

Allowing the land to "take a break" is sound agricultural practice. It is also healthy, both physically and emotionally, for the farmer—although it is far less healthy for the farmer's bank account.

The laws of *shemittah* seem to compound the difficulty. Not only is it forbidden to work the land in the seventh year, but the land and all its produce become ownerless for the duration of the year. Anyone and everyone, humans and animals, are equally entitled to enjoy what the Land of Israel brings forth.

It is therefore not difficult to understand why the laws of *shemittah* have historically been quite difficult to observe.

Parashat Vayelech

Farmers and, by extension, the entire economy were faced with a Herculean challenge, as the nation's finances shifted to "faith based economics." In a preindustrial society, alternative food sources were scarce, even nonexistent; the prospect of hardship must have been overwhelming, and the required level of faith in God extreme.

And yet, the sanctions and consequences spelled out by the Torah and the prophets are severe: Failure to observe the *shemittah* will result in exile.

No wonder, then, that at the end of the *shemittah* year, not unlike the end of Shabbat, our feelings are mixed. For some, a sigh of relief is in order—not only relief from the prohibitions and limitations on proactive working of the land, not only the rush of adrenaline that Israel's farmers feel as they are permitted to rekindle their active love affair with the land, but, in recent times, relief from the divisiveness that has come to be associated with *shemittah* observance.

There may be no area of Jewish law marked with as high a level of discord as *shemittah*, whose observance is marred by competing *kashrut* sensibilities that are often diametrically opposed to one another.

The irony is poignant, since even the most secular modern Israeli is familiar with the famous adage, borrowed from rabbinic commentary to the Torah, "What does *shemittah* have to do with Mount Sinai?" Today, this phrase usually points out that two subjects are completely unrelated, but a cynical reinterpretation of it may aptly describe today's *shemittah* observance: There is no connection between *shemittah*, the most fractious of all subjects, and Mount Sinai, where the nation stood "as one man, with one heart."

A Taste of Eden

Perhaps we can draw from another aspect of our weekly experience. As Shabbat wanes, we begin looking ahead to the next Shabbat. For some, these thoughts and musings are of a culinary nature: Which food or wine would we like to have at our next Shabbat table? Others look ahead to the social opportunities, planning who their next guests will be or with whom they would like to spend their next day of rest.

As the *shemittah* year comes to an end, we should be thinking along these same lines: How will the next sabbatical year look? What does *shemittah* mean in a modern, mainly non-agrarian, industrialized society? How can we make *shemittah* more relevant and more significant to our lives in the modern State of Israel? How can we improve the *shemittah* experience and reconnect with its original purpose? Can we find better ways to tap into the social underpinnings of these laws and apply them in a postindustrial economy? How can the benefits and the burdens of *shemittah* observance be shared among all sectors of society? Is there a way to apply debt cancellation, an integral part of *shemittah* observance, in our current financial system, and to allow Judaism's vision of social justice to help bridge the vast chasm between Israel's haves and have-nots? These are questions that we should address right now, as we end one *shemittah* cycle and begin again. If we put *shemittah* on the back burner and wait six years to ask these questions, it may be too late to formulate any meaningful response to the challenges and opportunities the sabbatical year holds in store.

As the *shemittah* year draws to a close, we would do well to ponder two diametrically opposed Talmudic teachings.

The first is dark and somewhat ominous:

Parashat Vayelech

In a discussion of the destruction of both the first and second Jewish commonwealths, the Sages note (*Ta'anit* 29a) that in both cases the destruction took place in the post-*shemittah* year. Apparently the Jewish people had not properly observed *shemittah*; society, unraveled from within by discord and disheartened by a lack of faith, was unable to withstand the external threats it faced.

However, on a more positive note, the Talmud (*Megillah* 17b) records a tradition that, ultimately, redemption will come at the end of the *shemittah* cycle. In a sense, this upbeat teaching is a challenge. Proper observance of *shemittah* creates social justice and unity, and these, without a doubt, are the key to our national and personal redemption.

This article originally appeared in The Jerusalem Post *(Metro & In Jerusalem sections), September 11, 2015. Reproduced with permission.*

Yom Kippur
"And Though the Holes Were Rather Small..."

In a daring and optimistic passage, the Rabbis describe the Divine assistance[58] received by those who make even the smallest gesture of repentance:

> R. Yassa said: The Holy One, blessed be He, said to Israel: My children, make for Me an opening of repentance no bigger than the point of a needle, and I will widen it for you into openings through which wagons and carriages can pass (*Shir ha-Shirim Rabbah* 5:3).

The Gaon of Vilna[59] focused on the odd language of this passage, which seems to be built upon a mixed metaphor: When referring to the eye of a needle, it would be more appropriate to use any of the words that denote a small gap, crack or hole. Instead, the word used is *petach* (opening), which is most commonly associated with an architectural gap such as a door or window.

---

58. Also see *Shabbat* 104a.
59. *Likkutei ha-Gra mi-Vilna, Moadim*, pp. 252f.

Alternatively, the contrast might have been drawn between the hole a pin leaves in a garment, rather than the eye of the needle, as compared to the wide gap created when a door is opened. The Gaon learned a very deep and significant lesson regarding repentance from the peculiar wording of this passage:

Sometimes, a small hole is of no significance. For example, when dough is left to rise, one may poke a hole in it that causes the dough to collapse, but the retreat is only temporary; soon enough, the dough will rise even higher than before. On the other hand, if one makes a hole in a garment—the hole is clear and permanent. The Gaon taught, based on this difference, that although God recognizes even the smallest gesture of repentance and responds with great largesse, man's gesture must be real, and not merely a fleeting, halfhearted gesture that leaves no impression on our own inner world.

The examples used by the Vilna Gaon to illustrate this teaching seem far from haphazard or coincidental. The first image, of dough as it rises, is an image familiar to readers of the Talmud as a metaphor for the evil inclination.[60] As dough becomes leavened, it expands and rises in a manner analogous to the human ego. Like the yeast in the mixture, sin draws all the other ingredients that comprise the human personality into the inflated sense of self-importance and self-sufficiency upon which the evil inclination feeds. Sticking a needle into the evil inclination, like poking a finger into a batch of rising dough, is a futile gesture; it makes a very temporary impression. This, the Gaon teaches us, is not the sort of repentant gesture that will stir God to come to our aid, to meet us along our path to

---

60. *Berachot* 17a.

repentance and guide us toward the light. Simply poking at the growing, festering mixture as it expands and rises actually helps the yeast work more effectively; this is not real *teshuvah*.

On the other hand, a hole made in a garment is qualitatively unlike a hole in rising dough; it is permanent, discernible—a proper *petach* or opening. This second image employed by the Gaon refers to a "*beged*," a word rooted in the Hebrew verb *begidah*, betrayal: The first clothing appeared after Adam and Eve ate from the forbidden tree and became suddenly aware of their nakedness. The clothing worn to cover their innocence is, therefore, both a consequence of sin and a sign of their rebellion, their betrayal of the trust God had placed in them, and their loss of innocence.

The fight against sin is a difficult battle, and the message the Vilna Gaon hoped to convey in this teaching is that we must be sincere, and make a real and discernible effort to change. Lip service or a bland poke at our own puffed-up egos will not suffice to convince God to come to our aid. Only when we feel the consequences of our own sin upon our shoulders, only when we become aware of how we have clothed ourselves in self-justification and continue to glorify our own rebellion,only when we make a hole in the garments of sin with which we cloak ourselves, will we be capable of breaking through and tapping into God's mercy. In a way, we may compare this hole to the tear a mourner makes in his or her garment, expressing a sense of loss and irreparable damage. And just as the torn garment cannot truly express the grief and pain of losing a loved one, the hole we make in our "clothing of sin" cannot fully express the remorse and shame that is the core of *teshuvah*. Even so, just as the smallest tear is a permanent sign of mourning, so too the

Yom Kippur

smallest hole in our tightly-woven web of ego and self-deception is guaranteed to arouse God's Mercy. Even a hole the size of a pinhead becomes the starting point for a new relationship with God. Through that small but permanent *petach*, a world of *teshuvah* is born.

Sukkot
Gatherings

Toward the end of the Torah, a rare commandment is presented; it is called *Hak'hel*, and refers to a mass gathering of the entire nation:

> Moshe then gave them the following commandment: At the end of every seven years, on the occasion of the *shemittah*, on the festival of Sukkot... you must read this Torah before all Israel, so that they will be able to hear it. You must gather together the people, the men, women, children and proselytes from your settlements, and let them hear it. They will thus learn to be in awe of the Almighty your God, carefully keeping all the words of this Torah. (*Devarim* 31:10-12)

Every seven years, a public gathering is to be held, a mass rally with the Torah at its center. At this event the Torah is to be read aloud so that all the people can hear, learn, and be inspired by the word of God. The image is exciting, energizing; what a wonderful mitzvah this must have been!

Sukkot

And yet, the timing specified in Moshe's instructions is intriguing: Why is this mitzvah fulfilled only once every seven years? Why at the end of the *shemittah* year? Why specifically on the holiday of Sukkot?

On the one hand we may posit that during the *shemittah* year, when all farming was suspended, the vast majority of society became full-time "yeshiva students." During their "sabbatical" from the arduous tasks and inflexible schedule of agricultural life, farmers were finally able to devote the time and energy to Torah study that they sorely lacked during the other six years of the cycle.[61] At the culmination of a year of study, the *Hak'hel* "rally" is a fitting final chord, a sort of closing ceremony for the year's spiritual and intellectual endeavors.

While this may explain the timing of *Hak'hel* at the end of the *shemittah* year, it does not explain the connection with the Sukkot festival. Although Sukkot is one of the three yearly festivals on which pilgrimage to Jerusalem is required, it is, in and of itself, a holiday replete with ceremony. Why add this additional mitzvah to an already-laden festival?

The Jewish holidays reflect the agricultural cycle of the Land of Israel, as well as the historical and theological foundations of Judaism. In fact, the festival we know as Sukkot is first introduced in the Torah[62] by its agricultural name, the Festival of the Harvest, without mention of its historical/theological significance. Interestingly, the Festival of the Harvest is presented in the context of the laws of *shemittah*:

---

61. See Hizkuni, *Devarim* 31:10; *Hadar Zekeinim, Devarim* 31:10; Ibn Ezra, *Devarim* 31:10; Ibn Ezra, *Shemot* 20:8.
62. *Shemot* 23:16.

A Taste of Eden

You may plant your land for six years and gather its crops. But during the seventh year, you must leave it alone and withdraw from it. The needy among you will then be able to eat [from your fields] just as you do, and whatever is left over can be eaten by wild animals. This also applies to your vineyard and your olive grove (*Shemot* 23:11).... Keep the Festival of Matzahs. Eat matzahs for seven days, as I commanded you, during the prescribed time in the spring, since this is when you left Egypt (*Shemot* 23:15). [Also keep] the Reaping Festival of the first fruits of your produce that you planted in the field. [There is also] the Harvest Festival at the end of the year, when you gather your produce from the field. (*Shemot* 23:16)

The historical/theological character of the Festival of Sukkot celebrates some very particular aspects of the Exodus:[63] When the Israelites left Egypt, they lived in the wilderness for forty years, protected and sustained by God. The huts we erect on Sukkot commemorate this spiritual and physical dependence on God, the temporary abodes of the desert and the Clouds of Glory with which God shielded us from harm.[64] As such, this festival could just as easily have been celebrated at any time of the year. On the other hand, the agricultural character of the holiday places it firmly at the end of the agricultural cycle, when the harvest is gathered from the fields.[65] This is the aspect of the festival referred to as *Chag ha-Asif*, the holiday of gathering.

---

63. *Vayikra* 23:43.
64. *Sukkah* 11b.
65. See Ibn Ezra, *Shemot* 23:16; *Ha-Ktav ve-ha-Kabbalah*, *Shemot* 23:16.

Sukkot

With this latter aspect of the festival in mind, the selection of Sukkot in the year immediately following *shemittah* as the holiday most appropriate for observing *Hak'hel* becomes far more intriguing. During the *shemittah* year, nothing is planted, and anything that grows on its own is made ownerless[66]:

God spoke to Moshe at Mount Sinai, telling him to speak to the Israelites and say to them: When you come to the land that I am giving you, the land must be given a rest period, a Sabbath to God. For six years you may plant your fields, prune your vineyards, and harvest your crops, but the seventh year is a Sabbath of Sabbaths for the land. It is God's Sabbath during which you may not plant your fields, nor prune your vineyards. Do not harvest crops that grow on their own and do not gather the grapes on your un-pruned vines, since it is a year of rest for the land. [What grows while] the land is resting may be eaten by you, by your male and female slaves, and by the employees and resident hands who live with you. All the crops shall [also] be eaten by the domestic and wild animals that are in your land. (*Vayikra* 25:1-7)

What sort of harvest festival can we possibly observe if there is nothing left in the fields to gather? How can we celebrate by gathering up our produce if all the produce has been declared ownerless? What can the farmer bring to the Beit HaMikdash if he did not work the fields all year, and anything that might have

---

66. *Shemot* 23:11: "But during the seventh year, you must leave it alone and withdraw from it. The needy among you will then be able to eat [from your fields] just as you do, and whatever is left over can be eaten by wild animals. This also applies to your vineyard and your olive grove."

grown has been consumed by any and all takers? Surely, the scheduling of *Hak'hel* at the end of the sabbatical year is quite precise,[67] and is intended to address these very issues. Rather than rejoicing, together with his family, with the produce he gathers from his fields, the farmer has shared his produce with one and all throughout the seventh year. Now, instead of gathering the bounty of the fields, the people are gathered together. Rather than rejoicing with the physical fruits of the year's labor, the festival will celebrate the fruits of the year's spiritual and intellectual labor.

By observing *Hak'hel* at the end of the *shemittah* year, specifically on Sukkot, we celebrate a different kind of Harvest Festival: On this very rare opportunity, we are able to more readily identify the agricultural aspects of Sukkot, the aspects encapsulated in the name *Chag ha-Asif*, precisely because the harvest it celebrates is not agricultural. At the end of the *shemittah* year, *Hak'hel* enables us to make a *"siyum"* as it were, for a year of study and spiritual growth. The opportunity presented by *Hak'hel* allows us to draw inspiration from the passing *shemittah* year, to allow the kinship and mutual responsibility that lie at the heart of the laws of *shemittah* to inspire us all for the next six years, and to allow the Torah that we learned during the sabbatical year to take root in our hearts.[68]

---

67. See comments of R. Chaim Palitiel to *Shemot* 23:16.
68. See comments of Rabbi S.R. Hirsch, and *Meshech Hochmah* on *Devarim* 31:10.

Parashat Ha'azinu
Imagine

As we move away from the High Holy Days and return to life as usual, should we be satisfied to return to our *status quo ante*? Perhaps the experience of Rosh Hashanah and Yom Kippur should not be limited to retrospection and stock-taking of the passing year. Instead, these days of introspection might equally be an opportunity for spiritual transformation. We might use them as a springboard for the year ahead, and come away from the holidays not as we were, but as a "new and improved model" of ourselves.

How can we achieve this? First and foremost, we might look to the Yom Kippur service itself for assistance. In addition, the Torah reading for the Shabbat immediately following the High Holy Days contains a message that we can apply in the days and weeks after the holiday season, a lesson that will enable us to descend from the heights of spirituality achieved during these unique days without sliding back to where we were before.

Parashat Ha'azinu is Moshe's parting song, and it is read each year during this period of heightened spiritual sensitivity. One particular verse, which has become an integral part of our liturgy, leads Rashi to connect the song of *Ha'azinu* to the service in the Beit HaMikdash:

A Taste of Eden

When I proclaim God's Name, praise God for His greatness. (*Devarim* 32:3)

In his comments on this verse, Rashi cites a Talmudic[69] teaching regarding the appropriate response to the recitation of a blessing. We are all familiar with the normal response to a blessing: "Amen." This short statement is both an affirmation of the content of the blessing itself and a testament to our shared belief in God. However, in the Beit HaMikdash, the response to a blessing was, "Blessed be His great Name (the Name of Kingship) forever and all time." This same response is recorded in the Yom Kippur liturgy in which we recount the Kohen Gadol's service in the Beit HaMikdash: When the Kohen Gadol uttered the ineffable Name of God, all those within earshot would fall on their knees, bow and prostrate themselves, and declare, "Blessed be His great Name (the Name of Kingship) forever and all time." Even today, this scene is reenacted in many congregations during the Yom Kippur recitation of the *Avodat Kohen Gadol*, despite the fact that the ineffable Name of God is no longer spoken.

The message we might take with us from this once-a-year experience lies in its uniqueness: In the course of our daily "non-Beit HaMikdash" life, we respond to blessings that include God's Name by saying "Amen." At no point in our lives is the ineffable Name of God spoken, nor is it our practice to kneel or prostrate ourselves in prayer. Despite this, we are reminded of what once was, of what should be, and what will be the proper order of things when the Beit HaMikdash is rebuilt; Yom Kippur helps us keep our sights on that other reality by transporting us to a

---

69. *Ta'anit* 16b.

Parashat Ha'azinu

different place and time—a place and time that once was, and will one day be again. On the holiest day of the year, we re-create the Beit HaMikdash experience, and we attempt to insert ourselves into that reality and imagine ourselves among those assembled in the courtyard of the Temple, bowing in awe as the Kohen Gadol declares God's omnipotence. If we are able to refer back to that experience whenever we hear a blessing, if we are able to make that other reality a part of our inner world, we can take the Yom Kippur experience with us through the rest of the year. Each time we answer "Amen," we have an opportunity to hear, in our innermost ear, to envision in our mind's eye, the response to a blessing uttered in the confines of the Beit HaMikdash: "Blessed be His great Name (the Name of Kingship) forever and all time."

Other elements of the Yom Kippur liturgy pose a similar challenge; most notable among these is the *Aleinu*, with which we conclude prayers throughout the year. Coming, as it does, at the end of every service, *Aleinu* "don't get no respect"; more often than not, *Aleinu* is mumbled in a rush as worshippers hurry out the door of the synagogue. However, on the High Holy Days, *Aleinu* has a central role in the liturgy. On Rosh Hashanah and Yom Kippur, *Aleinu* is recited slowly, deliberately, with great concentration and intent, at the very heart of the service. On these Days of Awe, *Aleinu* takes on an entirely different character: Worshippers bow and kneel as the words of this sublime prayer—which are exactly the same all year round—help them reach new heights of spirituality. Here, then is that same challenge: Can we muster the fervent intensity of the prayers of the High Holy days throughout the year? Can we recall the High Holy Days experience of *Aleinu* as

A Taste of Eden

we repeat this prayer three times daily throughout the year? The awe of Rosh Hashanah and Yom Kippur, as our lives hang in the balance, makes all our prayers more fervent, more intense, but spiritual awareness is not something we should reserve for ten days each year. Our challenge is to draw upon the holiness of the High Holy Days all year long. Perhaps our thrice-daily repetition of *Aleinu* can remind us of that challenge and help us rise to meet it.

We have the capacity to infuse our lives with holiness. To do so, all we have to do is utilize the greatest gift God gave us: the human imagination. If we use it to picture holiness, we can uplift our everyday lives and achieve new levels of spirituality.

Parashat VeZot HaBerachah
From Sinai to Jerusalem

In the final *parashah* of the Torah, Moshe takes leave of his people by blessing them:

And this is the blessing with which Moshe, the man of God, blessed the children of Israel [just] before his death. He said: "God came from Sinai and shone forth from **Se'ir** to them; He appeared from Mount **Paran**..." (*Devarim* 32:2)

As a preface to the blessings he is about to bestow upon them, Moshe makes reference to two specific geographical locations, two places that have been mentioned before but whose significance he does not explain: Se'ir and Paran. Rashi, drawing upon earlier traditions,[70] fills in the blanks for us:

"...and shone forth from Se'ir to them": [Why did He come from Se'ir?] Because God first offered the children of Esav [who dwelled in Se'ir] that they accept the Torah, but they did not want [to accept it].

---

70. See *Sifri*, *Devarim*, *VeZot HaBerachah*, *Piska* 343.

A Taste of Eden

"...from Mount Paran": [Why did God then come from Paran?] Because He went there and offered the children of Yishmael [who dwelled in Paran] to accept the Torah, but they [also] did not want [to accept it]. (Rashi, *Devarim* 32:2)

Rashi, always a sensitive reader of the text, explains these cryptic references to long-forgotten places through the application of a well-known tradition that has clear textual grounding: Yishmael, son of Hagar and Avraham, "settled in the Paran wilderness" after he and his mother were banished from Avraham's tent (*Bereishit* 21:21), while Esav's domain in Se'ir was well-known to this generation of Israelites, who had been instructed to steer well clear of the inheritance given to Yitzchak's other son (*Devarim* 2:5). Rashi deftly weaves the textual associations of Se'ir and Paran together with the tradition regarding their unwillingness to accept the Torah: Each of these sons of Avraham had been given the opportunity to become the People of the Book, as it were, but each had rejected the offer when they found out what was involved.

This approach stands in stark contrast to the approach of the Children of Israel. At the foot of Mount Sinai, when offered the Torah, they responded without hesitation, *naaseh ve-nishma*, "we will do and we will hear." They accepted the Torah "sight unseen," as it were, without question, without consideration of the pragmatics, of the demands that their acceptance of this Divine gift would entail.

The relationship between God and the Children of Israel is not dependent upon the content of the Torah; rather, the Torah is an expression of the unique relationship between them. This relationship isalso described by Rashi in the verse that prefaces Moshe's parting blessings:

> And this is the blessing with which Moshe, the man of God, blessed the children of Israel [just] before his death. He said: "God came from Sinai…"

> He came out toward them when they came to stand at the foot of the mountain, as a bridegroom goes forth to greet his bride, as it is said, "[And Moshe brought the people forth] toward God" (*Shemot* 19:17). We learn from this that God came out toward them. (Rashi, *Devarim* 32:2)

In a sense, when the Jews accepted the Torah, they entered into a covenant with God, taking a vow similar to those of marriage. When a man and woman are wed, they do not know what fortune (or perhaps misfortune) awaits; their future is a book that is as yet unwritten. Their marriage is not based upon any assurance of what the content of that book will be; it is based upon their love for one another, and the decision to share the journey into the unknown. Rashi contrasts the pragmatic relationship, the aborted relationship between God and the nations that live in Se'ir and Paran, with the loving relationship entered into by those who declared *naaseh ve-nishma*, who had no expectation of reading the content of the book before making the loving commitment to the future of their relationship. Esav and Yishmael demanded to read the fine print before entering into the covenant; what they read seemed to them excessively demanding, and they declined God's offer. The sons of Yaakov, on the other hand, had complete trust in the One who had offered them the covenant, and wanted nothing more than the loving relationship that this covenant would foster.

There may be a deeper level to this teaching: The names of the two protagonists, Esav and Yishmael, are suspiciously similar to the two words spoken by the children of Israel at the foot of Mount Sinai, *naaseh ve-nishma*, "we will do we will listen." Taking careful note of the roots of these Hebrew words unlocks layers of meaning that might be overlooked in translations: The word *naaseh*, "we will do," shares its root (*asah*) with the name Esav, while *nishma*, "we will listen," shares its root (*shama*) with the name Yishmael.[71]

There are several conclusions that we might draw from this etymological lesson: On the one hand, we might see within it an emphasis on the fidelity of the Jews versus the hesitation of those who perhaps might lay claim to some part of the inheritance of Avraham: The Children of Israel succeeded, in declaring *naaseh ve-nishma*, where the children of Esav and Yishmael had failed. Furthermore, we may say that in using these precise words, the Children of Israel channeled the spiritual power and potential that the others had forfeited.

On the other hand, as we approach the final verses of the Five Books of Moshe—and begin again, returning to Genesis, to *Bereishit*, to Creation, perhaps there is new hope. All of mankind was created in the image of God; the entire world was created with spiritual potential. The message of the last chapter

---

71. This teaching is found in the commentary of the Vilna Gaon in his *Aderet Eliyahu*, *Devarim* 32:2, and in numerous places in the writings of the Chida, who attributes the idea to the *Torat Chaim* commentary (authored by R. Abraham Hayyim ben R. Naftali Tzvi Hirsch Schor, d. 1632) on *Avodah Zarah* 2b.

Parashat VeZot HaBerachah

of *Devarim* leads directly to the message of the first chapter of *Bereishit*: those who succeeded in creating this unique, loving bond with God, and those who failed. We are given the opportunity to pause and wonder, to pause and hope, that the realty of the past does not dictate the destiny of the future. We do not rest on the laurels of the blessings of *VeZot HaBerachah* and the knowledge that our relationship with God is unique; instead, we wait for the day that all peoples of the earth will embrace the word of God and live in tranquility.

Also the strangers that join themselves to God to serve Him and to love the name of God, to be His servants... I will bring them to My holy mountain, and make them joyful in My house of prayer; their burnt-offerings and their sacrifices shall be acceptable upon My altar, for My house shall be called a house of prayer for all peoples. Thus declares the Almighty God who gathers the dispersed of Israel: Yet I will gather others to him, beside those that are gathered. (*Yishayahu* 56:6-8)

Chazak Chazak V'nitchazek!